THE
LIBRARY ASSISTANT'S
MANUAL

FOURTH EDITION

THE
LIBRARY ASSISTANT'S
MANUAL

FOURTH EDITION

F. John Chirgwin
formerly College Librarian
Stockport College of Further and Higher Education

LIBRARY ASSOCIATION PUBLISHING
LONDON

© F. John Chirgwin and Phyllis Oldfield 1978, 1982, 1988
© F. John Chirgwin and the Estate of Phyllis Oldfield 1993

Published by
Library Association Publishing Ltd
7 Ridgmount Street
London WC1E 7AE

First published 1978
Second edition 1982
Third edition 1988
This fourth edition 1993

British Library Cataloguing in Publication Data
Chirgwin, F. John
    Library Assistant's Manual. — 4Rev. ed
    I. Title II. Oldfield, Phyllis
    020

    ISBN 1-85604-071-2

Typeset from author's disks in 10/12pt Palatino by Saxon Graphics Ltd,
Derby.
Printed and made in Great Britain by Bookcraft (Bath) Ltd

In memory of Phyllis Oldfield

Contents

Preface

This book arose out of a course preparing candidates for the Library and Information Assistant's Certificate of the City and Guilds of London Institute. It was intended to be an introduction to elementary principles of librarianship for non-professional staff in libraries, and it sought to describe simple library routines in a non-technical manner. Now in its fourth revised edition, it has grown to become a simple introduction to libraries and librarianship for many people both in this country and abroad, forming a much wider audience than those who work in libraries.

It should still be useful for anyone studying for the Library and Information Assistant's Certificate, the BTEC double-option module on Library and Information Work, those engaged upon in-service training courses, and people contemplating a career in libraries, although it has changed from being a 'how to' book, and is now more of a general survey.

In the fourth edition, the text has been completely revised and updated, and there are two completely new chapters on 'Organizations and associations' and on 'Multi-media and information technology'. There are new sections on national libraries, equal opportunities, changes to local government in England, advice centres, the Net Book Agreement, binding; and some older material has been deleted.

The selection of assignments at the end of each chapter has been abandoned in line with the book's move away from a study text, and further reading has been added to each chapter, with a revised general reading list at the end of the book.

This is the first time that I have had to revise the book on my own, as sadly Phyllis Oldfield died last year, and it was a much longer and more demanding task than I thought when I began. I hope I have overhauled it properly. My wife Mary, who is

Librarian at Lady Manners School, Bakewell in Derbyshire, has contributed many helpful suggestions, and has helped with typing and proof-reading. Diana Hough has also helped with typing.

John Chirgwin
October 1992.

List of abbreviations

AACR	Anglo-American Cataloguing Rules
AAL	Association of Assistant Librarians
Aslib	The Association for Information Management (formerly ASLIB: Association of Special Libraries and Information Bureaux)
ASSIA	*Applied social sciences index and abstracts*
AV	Audiovisual
BHI	*British humanities index*
BL	British Library
BLAISE	British Library Automated Information Service
BLCMP	Birmingham Libraries Cooperative Mechanization Project
BLDSC	British Library Document Supply Centre
BLISS	British Library Information Sciences Service
BNB	*British national bibliography*
BS(I)	British Standards (Institution)
BT	British Telecom
BTEC	Business and Technology Education Council
BUFVC	British Universities Film and Video Council
CAB	Citizen's Advice Bureau(x)
CANS	Citizen's Advice Notes Service
CATNI	*Catchword and trade name index*
CD	Compact disc
CD-ROM	Compact disc – read only memory
CGLI	City and Guilds of London Institute
CIP	Cataloguing in publication
CLA	Copyright Licensing Agency
CNAA	Council for National Academic Awards
COMLA	Commonwealth Libraries Association
CTI	*Current technology index*

DDC	Dewey Decimal Classification
DFE	Department for Education
DNH	Department for National Heritage
DPR	Data Protection Registry
DSS	Department of Social Security
DTP	Desktop publishing
ECCTIS	Educational Counselling and Credit Transfer Information Service
ERA	Education Reform Act
FE	Further education
FEFC	Further Education Funding Council
GCSE	General Certificate of Secondary Education
HELPIS	Higher Education Learning Programmes Information Service
HMI	Her Majesty's Inspector(ate)
HMSO	Her Majesty's Stationery Office
IFLA	International Federation of Library Associations
ISBN	International Standard Book Number
ISSN	International Standard Serial Number
IT	Information technology
LA	Library Association
LAR	*Library Association record*
LEC	Local Enterprise Companies
LIBS	Library and Information Briefings Series
LISA	*Library and information science abstracts*
LISC	Library and Information Services Council
LMS	Local Management of Schools
LRDG	Learning Resources Development Group
MARC	Machine-readable catalogue
NACAB	National Association of Citizen's Advice Bureaux
NBA	Net Book Agreement
NCET	National Council for Educational Technology
NCVQ	National Council for Vocational Qualifications
NERIS	National Educational Resources Information Service
NLB	National Library for the Blind
NVQ	National Vocational Qualification
OED	*Oxford English dictionary*
OPAC	Online public access catalogue

OU	Open University
PLR	Public lending right
RLB	Regional Library Bureau
SCET	Scottish Council for Educational Technology
SCONUL	Standing Conference of National and University Libraries
SCOTVEC	Scottish Vocational Education Council
SINTO	Sheffield Interchange Organization
SLA	School Library Association
SVQ	Scottish Vocational Qualification
TEC	Training and Enterprise Council
TEED	Training Education and Enterprise Directorate
UDC	Universal Decimal Classification
UNESCO	United Nations Educational, Scientific and Cultural Organization
VDU	Visual display unit
WBIP	*Whitaker's books in print*

1

Public libraries

The Public Libraries (England) Act of 1850 allowed the establishment of town libraries, which were provided by funds from local
rates and were free and open to all ratepayers. Because the right
to establish such a library on the part of any municipal authority
was permissive and not compulsory, many years elapsed before
the entire needs of all the potential reading public across the
country were realized.

A further Act, the Public Libraries Act of 1919, gave the
opportunity for greatly increased library provision, empowering
county councils to adopt the Libraries Act for those districts
within their respective areas which had not already done so. The
new county library systems established buildings for branch
libraries within their respective areas, in the small towns and
large villages where no libraries had previously existed. Even in
small villages and hamlets, centres were set up in school rooms or
other suitable existing buildings, where regular exchanges of
book stock housed at headquarters could be arranged. These
libraries were, and still are, organized from a county headquarters, normally sited in the county town.

The passing of the Public Libraries and Museum Act 1964
meant that for the first time all parts of England and Wales were
given as of right a comprehensive and nationally linked library
service. With local government reorganization in 1974 came
changes in the boundaries of public library authorities. Some
county branch libraries were transferred to adjacent municipal
authorities, and became branch libraries served by the central
library of the municipal authority, instead of, as formerly, by the
county headquarters. But whether under the auspices of a county
or municipal authority, and of whatever size or type, all public
libraries continue as the Kenyon Report (1927) proposed that they

should: 'to serve not only the earnest seekers after knowledge, but also all those who are ... gratifying an elementary curiosity and those who are seeking relaxation and recreation'.

Purpose

Public libraries generally have been established and developed to fulfil four main purposes.

Firstly, they exist to provide educational support at every level, from pre-school through primary, secondary and further education, and even for university undergraduates and adult education classes. In fact students of the Open University must rely heavily on public library resources since the OU Library does not cater for undergraduates, but only for staff. Of course public libraries provide educational support in a general way, and are rarely a substitute for academic libraries. However, they often provide materials on most subjects at every level. They are useful for background or marginal material, and they are a gateway to the network of national library resources provided for all.

Secondly, public libraries provide information. This service is usually undertaken by reference libraries at specialist subject departments in large city libraries. Enquiries are answered in person, by post, telephone or by the most up-to-date electronic means. Again, public libraries are the access point to the wider information world, and enquiries are rarely left unanswered, although they may be passed on to further specialist sources. In rural areas, the public library is often the only source of true, unbiased information, and public libraries have a difficult job providing information and reference services to small populations covering large areas.

Thirdly, public libraries support leisure and recreational activities; and by fostering reading as a pastime they promote the growth of a healthy and enlightened population. Many public libraries provide books and periodicals on gardening, sporting activities and fiction. They provide musical recordings, feature films on video, and computer games. For older people and the housebound these services can be valuable socially as well as in a recreational sense.

Lastly, they provide support for cultural and artistic activities, promoting an interest in and love of literature, drama, the arts, music and dance. Public libraries do this by supplying books, journals and audiovisual media, and also by providing a range of extension activities such as exhibitions, lectures, performances, and festivals. Some large city libraries run library theatre companies, and many children's library services provide puppet shows and street theatre activities. Many public libraries provide premises for artistic performances and meetings to take place and they often provide a well developed focus for local societies and organizations.

Location

It is essential that public libraries are sited centrally in their respective cities, towns or villages, preferably on or near main roads which give access to public transport, and where car-parking facilities can be made available. Many central libraries are now built adjacent to or as an integral part of shopping centres. In this way it is easier for libraries to attract and retain their borrowing public.

Similarly, branch libraries are sited centrally in their respective smaller towns and villages, offering a representative though necessarily more limited selection of library services to their borrowers. Such libraries act as access points to the full range of resources that are housed in the central libraries with which they are linked. In the same way, mobile libraries serve the needs of readers living in the more remote areas, giving such people entry as of right into all regional and national resources.

It has become the practice for libraries to make lecture and meeting rooms available to serve the needs of the local community, and to support an immense variety of extension activities. In many directions therefore, the library, in the various purposes it serves, becomes the focal point and cultural centre of its own neighbourhood.

The lending department

A good first impression of the library often stems from the tactful ways in which well trained library assistants can provide information and help with membership formalities. Some people appreciate being taken on a quick tour of the library by the library assistant, who is able to point out where their special-interest areas are to be found. For those who prefer to explore the library for themselves, a wall plan of the library floor, or floors, should be provided. In addition, a printed floor plan can be incorporated into a handout or guide which is made available to all new library members.

It is becoming increasingly common for school classes to visit their public library where they are taught, amongst other skills, how to handle the catalogue for themselves, and also how subjects are interrelated. This area of work could well be extended: many older people and others, such as the unemployed with more leisure time available, would welcome talks on how to use their library and its resources to the full.

The larger public libraries aim to provide a readers' advisory service point, where the borrowers' specific information needs can be met. Here all the bibliographical aids are to hand, to enable the adviser to answer questions concerning titles of books in print and of newly published books not held in the library. Many libraries pride themselves on supplying book lists of special categories of books. Often a library will compile its own book list on a topical theme, thus highlighting books that otherwise might remain unnoticed and unknown in their normal sequence on the shelves.

Another way in which libraries can highlight particular categories of books and thus demonstrate a theme that is common to all of them, is by mounting displays. Displays demonstrate interrelationships between subjects more directly, and with greater impact, than can the library catalogue. Displays can also link a library and its books with the outside world and its variety of other media. Readers are given the opportunity to broaden and deepen their interest, through having their attention drawn to books that have formed the basis of radio or television broadcasts. Again, displays planned to coincide with local events draw attention to other community activities, giving opportunities to demonstrate the connections linking the many and varied local recreational, cultural and educational activities.

Many libraries amass a considerable amount of community literature, some of which is kept on permanent display. Examples of such literature are careers information, educational courses handouts, and information handouts on where to go for advice and assistance of all kinds. Smaller libraries sometimes provide a diary which can be used by local organizations to publicize their own events and activities and which is particularly useful for new members of the community to consult. Further demands are now being made on public library resources and study accommodation by the number of open- and distance-learning programmes now being developed. One of the earliest of these was the Open University, which aims to extend and widen educational opportunities for mature adults. Public library opening hours are now having to be made more flexible to meet the demands of such working students.

Increasingly, attention is being paid to the needs of particular client groups which public libraries serve, in order to ensure the provision of appropriate, relevant services. This has resulted in many constructive developments in what is now referred to as 'community librarianship'. Such libraries now offer advice on benefits, employment, careers, housing, pensions, consumer affairs and other similar matters, or put people in touch with other sources.

The lending departments of the larger public libraries are increasingly offering items other than books for loan; the most common being pictures, records, audio cassettes, CDs, computer software and video recordings. It is usual to allow pictures to be kept by one borrower for a period of roughly three months and to make a small charge for each picture that is lent. Some libraries issue records, cassette tapes and CDs free of charge whilst others ask for a small fee per item borrowed, or else offer an annual subscription rate which covers the cost of borrowing any number of items within one year. Do-it-yourself language kits of open-learning materials are also offered on loan for use at home, or on the library premises.

The reference department

Public libraries also provide a reference department or, in the case of smaller libraries, a reference section. Books and other material provided here must of necessity be on hand for consultation at any time; therefore they are not as a rule available for loan. This department will house books of a general nature that deal with many subjects, such as encyclopaedias and collections of newspaper cuttings. It will also house books that for a variety of reasons cannot be allowed out on loan. Rare books, certain large-size books, e.g. atlases and collections of photographs, expensive books, out-of-print and irreplaceable works can all come into the category of 'reference books'; as can standard works on specialist subjects which people may wish to consult rather than read from cover to cover. In the interests of economy, large reference departments are increasingly drawing on a variety of computerized systems for the retrieval of information requested by users.

The reference department is also the one which holds local history collections, consisting not only of books but in addition old maps, documents, cuttings collections, guide books, booklets and pamphlets. Archives, i.e. local records and other manuscript documents relating to local institutions, may form part of such a collection. Current local information is also kept on file, and lists of addresses of local government departments, religious and social bodies and societies.

Publications issued by government departments, statistical information, and Acts of Parliament can all be consulted. Hansard, which is the official report of debates that have taken place in Parliament, is available at least in the large reference departments. In addition, the reference department – unless the library is large enough to warrant the provision of a separate commercial and technical department – will also contain all the appropriate quick-reference material which will include telephone, street and trade directories, bus, train and air timetables, yearbooks, gazetteers, guide books and bibliographical aids of all kinds. Effective use of all these reference sources can only be made after training and much practice. Library assistants should aim to develop an awareness of the source materials available, a knowledge of what they contain and the ability to locate quickly the particular items of information that are required. (See Chapter 11 for examples of reference materials.)

Commercial and technical departments

The central public library located in a large town or city generally provides an additional department usually known as the commercial and/or technical department. This serves the needs of commerce and industry in the area as well as the needs of individual citizens. Information seekers in this department are likely to request very specific items of information, and many enquiries are made and dealt with over the telephone.

The commercial department carries company information of all kinds concerning locally based firms, and also national ones and their subsidiaries. The quick-reference material such as trade directories, timetables and yearbooks are to hand in this department. Collections of materials relating to other countries, particularly in Europe, notably in the areas of industry, commerce and travel, are also available. Specialist information of concern to companies is supplied, including works on company law, patent specifications of recent inventions and British Standard specifications relating to manufactured products. Large-scale maps and street plans of the locality and surrounding areas may be consulted.

This is generally the department where current and back copies of daily, Sunday and local newspapers are kept, along with a range of magazines, journals and periodicals, of both a specialist and a general nature. Newspaper provision aims to cover a balanced political spectrum, whilst magazines and journals are reviewed from time to time to ensure the broadest possible range of professional and recreational reading. Back copies of newspapers and periodicals are held for a specified period, usually ranging from one to five years according to the lasting value of their contents. Most quality newspapers are now available on microfilm, and on CD-ROM. The most important periodicals of all are bound into yearly volumes which become part of the permanent book stock. To enable the borrower to trace articles relating to specific topics from periodicals and magazines, appropriate indexes, e.g. *Current technology index*, should be to hand. Once such an article has been traced, it is usually possible for the borrower to obtain photocopies of any articles, since photocopiers are now usually considered an essential feature of such a department. Some departments also provide the reader with printers which give copies of material in microfiche and microfilm form.

The children's department

The children's department has first to satisfy the recreational and leisure needs of its readers by offering a wide-ranging and well balanced fiction, non-fiction and reference book stock. It often augments the educational resources which are available to the child in school and elsewhere, through the provision of both book and non-book materials. Very young children accompanied by parents on visits, are given picture books to handle and to take home on loan. Books are placed in low-standing browser boxes in strategic corners of the main lending department or else in the children's department itself. The provision of low chairs or floor cushions encourages children to become naturally at ease in the library. Story-telling and story-reading sessions are arranged for pre-school children, and these draw attention to the connection between the spoken and the written word.

Although school is the place where the majority of children learn the mechanics of reading, not all schools are in a position to provide the wide range of imaginative, stimulating story books needed to encourage the children to put their newly acquired reading skills to the fullest use. Likewise many secondary schools, whilst providing non-fiction books appropriate to the school curriculum, do not always provide the spread of fiction that would be appropriate in order to cater fully for the needs of their particular pupils. There is a special onus therefore on the public library to provide the fullest possible coverage of good children's literature.

Children's and young people's services librarians, through their skilled selection of books and other resources, aim to ensure not only that their stocks develop and continue to be maintained to the highest standards, but also that children are made aware of what is available to them. Children's Book Weeks are promoted both nationally and locally, when exhibitions, competitions, and a variety of activities are arranged. Children's authors and illustrators are invited to come along, and to share their own world with their young audiences. Such promotions do much to encourage children to join their local public library; and so do events that are organized during school holiday times by the children's library staff. Many libraries now promote the services they offer through the sale of a variety of items such as T-shirts, bookmarks, pens, booklists and the like, to which are added appropriate captions, thus producing an extra source of revenue. A variety of extension activities, such as book clubs, competitions and quizzes, also helps to publicize the stock and the work of the department.

A children's reference section has always traditionally been headed by a selection of the best children's encyclopaedias.

Nowadays information exists in increasing quantity and comes from a variety of sources through an ever-increasing range of media. It is widely recognized that pupils must learn how to learn, and that a central feature of this process is knowing how to deal with information. For this reason, many more demands are now being made on the public library, its resources and its staff. Children at both primary and secondary level are being asked to carry out projects and assignments which involve them in both searching out and processing relevant information. Some libraries build up their own kits to help children in their search for information. These comprise not only newspaper cuttings, but also photographs, maps, charts, photocopies of letters and documents all relating to one theme.

With the introduction of the General Certificate of Secondary Education (GCSE), vocational courses, and the National Curriculum which will be followed by most school pupils, even greater demands will be made on all types of library resources. Of particular importance will be collections of up-to-date information on a wide range of topics. These will necessitate the provision of cuttings files for ephemeral material, microfiche, online links to external computer databases such as Prestel and Campus 2000, statistical data, video recordings, audio tapes and computer software. The information management skills of the librarians will be much in demand, as the National Curriculum becomes established, in the planning and provision of appropriate resource facilities and services, and in the professional assistance given to both teaching staff and pupils.

These then are the main ways in which the public library aims to satisfy the explicit needs of its wide-ranging readership. A forward-looking library, however, must not fail to be constantly exploring new developments in areas for which the library has not hitherto made provision.

Further reading

Benge, R.C., *Libraries and cultural change*, Bingley, 1986 [1970].

Kelly, T., *History of public libraries in Great Britain, 1845–1975*, 2nd edn, LA, 1977.

Murison, W.J., *The public library: its origins, purpose and significance*, 3rd rev.edn, Bingley, 1988.

Usherwood, R., *The public library as public knowledge*, LA, 1988.

2

National and academic libraries

National libraries

National libraries exist to gather, store and preserve the publishing output of a country. Many are copyright or legal-deposit libraries, which means they are entitled by law to receive a free copy of all material published in their respective countries. In the UK, legal deposit is covered by the Copyright (Libraries) Act 1911, which designated the following libraries as copyright libraries:

The British Museum Library (now part of the British Library)
National Library of Scotland
National Library of Wales
Bodleian Library (library of Oxford University)
Cambridge University Library
Library of Trinity College Dublin (NB Ireland was not a republic then).

These libraries undertake to classify, catalogue and preserve such material, and make it available. The recording of material acquired under legal deposit is often used to prepare the national bibliography, which can be used as the basis for book selection by other libraries.

National libraries provide for the development and coordination of national policy on research and development in library matters. They also serve in the capacity of national agents in the field of international library cooperation. The Office for International Lending of the International Federation of Library Associations and Institutions which administers an international lending system is based at the British Library Document Supply Centre at Boston Spa.

The British Library is said to be one of the world's largest national libraries. Other large examples are the United States Library of Congress, the Russian State Library, and the French Bibliothèque Nationale, and as these are among the oldest national libraries consequently they have the largest collections. The British Library was established by Act of Parliament in 1973, by amalgamating the former British Museum Library with the National Central Library, the National Lending Library for Science and Technology and the British National Bibliography.

The British Library has a complex structure with several divisions and departments:

The Corporate Services section comprises the Chief Executive's Office, finance, marketing, public relations and central administration including such functions as personnel and buildings.

The Humanities and Social Services Division comprises the Department of Printed Books, the Department of Manuscripts, and the Department of Oriental Manuscripts and Printed Books. This Division also includes the India Office Library, the collections of maps, music, newspapers, postage stamps, and ephemera such as postcards, posters and greetings cards. Also included is the National Sound Archive which aims to preserve all kinds of recorded music and wildlife sounds.

The Science Technology and Industry Division covers the Science Reference and Information Service and the Document Supply Centre at Boston Spa which is concerned specifically with interlending and whose work is more fully described in Chapter 9. The Science Reference and Information Service covers the former Science Reference Library and the old Patent Office Library, and holds the major UK reference collection of scientific and technological literature.

The Research and Development Department encourages and supports library and information research and its dissemination, by funding projects and publishing the results.

The Bibliographic Services Division's role is to record a wide selection of the printed material acquired by the Library, to provide online computer services such as BLAISE-LINE and BLAISE-LINK, to supply catalogue records in a variety of formats to other libraries, and to arrange courses and visits for librarians and other interested persons. It publishes the *British national bibliography*, *Books in English*, the *British catalogue of music* and *Serials in the British Library*, thus giving the widest possible coverage of UK publishing output.

In order to meet the requirements of a national library for the 21st century, a new building is under construction for central London, at St Pancras, which will re-house many of the British Library's reference collections under one roof. The Document Supply Centre and the Publications Sales Unit will continue to operate from Boston Spa in Yorkshire.

The National Library of Scotland, at Edinburgh, has a very large collection on Scottish history and genealogy. The Scottish Central Library was merged in 1974 and became the Lending Services Division, responsible for library interlending in Scotland.

The National Library of Wales, at Aberystwyth, collects material on Welsh language, literature, history and culture. It is responsible for library interlending in Wales.

The National Library for the Blind (NLB) is an independent library funded by subscriptions, legacies and grants. It produces books, magazines, and other materials of a general nature in braille, Moon or large-print versions, and lends them to blind or visually handicapped people, through public libraries acting as agents, or through the post to individuals.

University libraries

Some universities are hundreds of years old and others have developed over the last 40 to 50 years. Recently, the Further and Higher Education Act 1992 has elevated the former polytechnics to university status. So there is great diversity of provision, in both the size and content of university libraries. This great expansion has brought problems in building collections of material to support the teaching and research needs of greatly increased numbers of students and staff. Many new university libraries have been built, but despite this there have been problems over the availability of material, limitations on the space available, and the financial resources to enable solutions to be found. Suggested options have included setting limits for bookstock by discarding material at the same rate as additions to stock, by more cooperation in stockholding, and more reliance on British Library provision.

University libraries will normally provide a range of textbooks and background reading to support the teaching and the courses undertaken there. They will also build up special collections to support the research work of the university. There will be archive and manuscript material, and a collection of theses submitted by postgraduate students and members of staff. Theses are written reports on the progress made and conclusions arrived at after research has been completed. They are not widely available, and can cause problems of bibliographical control and accessibility. Journals are very important because they are the accepted medium for conveying news of research findings and up-to-date information. In addition to strong collections of journals, most of the relevant abstracting and indexing services will be available so that research workers can keep abreast of all the work that is going on in a particular area of study. University libraries will have comprehensive collections of bibliographical material, including foreign literature and historical material.

Most university libraries will prepare printed guides to their collections, explaining the layout and contents of the library, and the services provided. The guide will explain how the collection is classified and catalogued; and provide help on how readers may find their material easily and quickly.

Large university libraries can be housed on different floors, or in other departmental buildings, and so using the catalogue is very important, especially to locate special collections which may be housed separately. Bibliographical materials are usually shelved beside the catalogues, and increasingly these days many of the bibliographical databases and catalogues are prepared by computer and are available online.

User education programmes are now commonplace, and extend beyond explaining how to use the library, to literature-searching techniques and the use of the main bibliographies, abstracts, indexes and reference works in specialized areas. Library staff work closely with academic teaching staff, and many libraries appoint staff to liaise formally with teaching faculties on matters such as book selection, short-loan collections and the improvement of services generally. Most university library staff will be subject specialists.

A feature of university libraries is the provision of study places for long periods, and so most libraries will be open from 9 a.m. to 10 p.m. on weekdays, with probably shorter hours at weekends and in vacations. Where sources are recommended for the completion of assignments, it is important that students should not keep books longer than necessary, and so many libraries arrange short loans, for as little as two hours in some cases, and charge heavy fines to act as a deterrent to defaulters, and to ensure that all students have a fair chance of access to the required reading.

The university library should build collections to support the teaching and research being undertaken, including bibliographical keys to material available elsewhere. These collections should be organized so as to allow easy access to their contents. Library resources and services should be publicized, and user education programmes should be available to all. The library buildings should be designed and arranged to permit these functions to happen easily. There should be well qualified staff to give direction and to liaise with their teaching colleagues in achieving this.

College libraries

The Further and Higher Education Act 1992 has removed further education and sixth-form colleges from local authority control into independent corporations funded centrally by the Further Education Funding Council, and other sources such as Training and Enterprise Councils, and Local Enterprise Companies.

Many colleges serve an ever-changing population of full-time, part-time, day-release, sandwich-course and evening-class students. College courses are closely associated with the needs of local industry, commerce and the professions, and they are increasingly concerned with developing skills and competences for the world of work. Courses on offer cover a wide range of vocational subjects, GCSE and A-level subjects, BTEC National and Higher National Certificates and Diplomas, professional courses for nurses, designers, managers and others, and in some cases, higher education diplomas and degrees. The 1992 Act has abolished the Council for National Academic Awards, and colleges have now made arrangements for their higher education work to be validated and supported or franchised by universities or other training bodies. This has been mutually helpful, since the universities are assured of a steady stream of recruits to their degree courses, and they can also give tangible help and support to FE colleges, for instance by permitting access to library facilities, in ways that CNAA was never able to offer. The Training Education and Enterprise Directorate, formerly the Manpower Services Commission, promotes and supports a number of courses for the unemployed and/or school leavers, and Training and Enterprise Councils and Local Enterprise Companies are also very active in this field.

There has been an increasing awareness of flexible ways of delivering the curriculum, with attention on open and distance learning and Open College courses. This widening of access for people who do not wish to attend traditional college courses is now bringing influence to bear on the whole FE curriculum. Courses are more modular. There is more accreditation for prior learning and experience. Students follow individual learning programmes at their own pace, using flexible learning materials and drawing on library materials in a variety of ways. College staff offer counselling and tutorial services on an individual basis, by telephone or correspondence where necessary. Vocational qualifications are being revised by the National Council for Vocational Qualifications and SCOTVEC, who are introducing a range of NVQs and SVQs at different levels to assess and accredit competences and the quality of skills achieved, rather than knowledge gained.

College libraries must aim to cover this range of subjects, levels and styles of learning. They must provide knowledge and information on traditionally taught courses, with general and reference material and bibliographical aids for books and journals. Much material is now presented in microfiche, audiovisual or computerized formats, so students must be taught to operate the various types of equipment. User education and study skills teaching is essential for the newer styles of learning programmes. Most college libraries will also aim to provide a selection of general background reading and current affairs, recreational reading and English and foreign fiction to cover general, complementary or communications studies. Business and Technology Education Council (BTEC) courses are well established in colleges now, and their project-, assignment- and information-based problem-solving approach has played a major part in the delivery of these courses, making increasing demands on college library resources.

Audiovisual media and information technology are now provided on such a scale that many colleges house and administer them in a separate AV workshop or resource centre. Other colleges retain direct links by housing and managing libraries, resource centres and learning workshops together. Colleges often serve their local communities by making their resources available to local business organizations and industrial firms, and by supplying technical literature and information on request. Several colleges have developed close links with local employers by appointing liaison or development officers to promote this aspect of their work.

School libraries

There is little national direction or implementation of agreed policy for school libraries, and consequently there are wide variations in the ways they are financed and staffed, leading to uneven provision.

Public libraries have always given support to school libraries, especially in county or rural areas, in addition to their provision for children and young people. Many good school libraries have been established and developed through the hard work and enthusiasm of school teachers and librarians who work with children and young people, and through the cooperation which takes place between these people and the organizations they represent.

Schools Library Services

It is almost impossible for a school library to be self-sufficient in terms of the materials needed to support the curriculum, and so many local authorities have set up Schools Library Services to act as supporting agencies for schools. Such a service is probably the most cost-effective way of providing the full range of learning materials and professional advice to a large number of schools over a large or densely populated area.

Schools Library Services have three main functions: to provide services and materials to the schools; to give professional advice to the schools; and also to supply feedback from the schools to the local authority. Services to schools include access to a wide range of learning materials to enhance the schools' own resources, project and topic collections, access to bibliographical sources, databases and IT support, display materials, exhibition and promotional help with special events, and help with book selection in the form of exhibition collections of new books which can be inspected and assessed at first hand before purchase.

Professional advice to schools includes support on the management and organization of school libraries, recruitment of staff, monitoring and evaluation, policy creation and assistance with budget preparation. Support to the local authority will be concerned with maintaining a level of provision across the authority, particularly at a time of curriculum or organizational change, fostering links with the advisory service and public library services and those with other departments such as museums and historic buildings. Schools Library Services do more than just provide additional materials, and the better ones can point to a continuing record of achievement in contributing to the success of the learning programme.

As a result of the Education Reform Act 1988, schools now have independent control of their budgets, and under Local Management of Schools (LMS) they can decide whether or not to purchase central services such as school library support. In a time of great change in the curriculum, the value of such services would seem to be obvious, but financial decisions are being made separately in each school as to whether or not to buy in this service. The future of many Schools Library Services is in the balance.

Curriculum support

A recent HMI survey entitled 'Better libraries: good practice in schools' (1989) contains the following statement: 'There are important implications for library provision in the development of an effective National Curriculum. The objectives of the National Curriculum will be best supported in those schools which have a broad, balanced and up to date provision of library books and resource materials.' It is important that the learning materials available in school libraries should be part of a well organized collection, so as to form a sound basis for curriculum

17

work to proceed. This is best achieved by the appointment of chartered librarians. There are not many dually qualified teacher librarians, although their numbers are increasing.

Much recent curriculum development has encouraged more emphasis on acquiring skills than on knowledge, and so skills such as information gathering and problem solving have become much more important. There is also much more emphasis on working independently, or in flexible modes, where learners work at their own pace either individually or in small groups. This emphasis on the child learning – rather than the teacher teaching – makes obvious demands on school libraries when project work and discovery methods are used.

Hand in hand with good school libraries with a wide range of multi-media and resource-based learning material available, should go the skills needed to make the most of what *is* available. Traditionally, user education and library skills have been taught together. Now they are seen as a much wider range of skills, which ideally should be integrated across the curriculum.

Further reading

British Library, *Gateway to knowledge: the British Library strategic plan, 1989–1994*, BL, 1989.

Day, A., *The British Library: a guide to its structure, publications, collections and services*, LA, 1988.

Department of Education and Science, *Better libraries, good practice in schools: a survey by H.M. Inspectorate*, HMSO, 1989.

Leach, A., 'The National Library for the Blind', *British journal of visual impairment*, Spring, 1985, 11–13.

Library Association, *Learning resources in schools: Library Association guidelines for school libraries*, LA, 1992.

Library Association, COFHE Group, *Guidelines for college and polytechnic libraries*, 4th edn, LA, 1990.

Line, M. and Line, J., *National libraries*, Library Information Technology Centre, 1992 (LIBS no. 32).

McElroy, A.R., *College librarianship*, LA, 1984.

Pack, P.J. and Pack, F.M., *Colleges, learning and libraries*, Bingley, 1985.

School libraries: the foundations of the curriculum. Report of the LISC working party, HMSO, 1984.

School Library Association, *School libraries: steps in the right direction*, SLA, 1989.

Stirling, J.F., *University librarianship*, LA, 1981.

Thompson, J. and Carr, R., *Introduction to university library administration*, 4th edn., Bingley, 1987.

3

Special libraries and information centres

Special libraries cover a wide range of library services providing current, detailed information for specialist users, often in a clearly defined subject area. They are primarily for the use of staff or research workers. They cover information based on collections of journal literature with the necessary abstracting and indexing services, standards, patents, legal and commercial information, and statistical and economic data.

There are many government libraries which fall into this category, such as the House of Commons Library, or the libraries of ministries and departments. Some are quite large, and most are very specialized. The libraries of public corporations, such as British Rail and many hospital libraries, are important special libraries, used primarily by employees and technical staff. The libraries of industrial firms, like ICI and British Aerospace, provide specialized material for technical staff and research workers. Many such firms are working at the frontiers of knowledge in their field, and up-to-date, authoritative, detailed information is essential for their continued progress and corporate success. Many professional or commercial organizations maintain libraries as a service to their members and practitioners, operating postal services throughout the UK and sometimes abroad. These libraries are biased towards a particular professional or vocational body of knowledge and practice.

The collections held in special libraries will be subject specific and very detailed, and will cover the widest possible range of material in the relevant areas. Much of the material will be in journal form, or what is known as grey literature – semi-published reports, government documents, theses, ephemera and conferences, trade literature, press cuttings and foreign material. Access to journals is important, and so those that are not taken will be carefully monitored through abstracts, indexes and *Current contents*, before obtaining relevant material from BLDSC or via local or trade information networks. Access to online databases via computer is also very common.

An important part of a special librarian's job will be to disseminate information in a proactive way, and so many special libraries prepare current awareness bulletins or individually tailored services to staff. Often they undertake literature searches and become quite skilled at seeking out and presenting information for others. Special library staff are usually subject specialists. Aslib is very prominent as a coordinating body for staff engaged upon this type of work. From time to time there have been moves to integrate their work with mainstream librarianship, but the very nature of their specialized work has prevented this from happening, except in a very general way. More than ever it has become apparent that people working in special libraries have acquired knowledge and skills which require more detailed training and support that traditional librarianship offers only sparingly, although the tendency for both parts of the profession to become more concerned with automated and computer-based systems and techniques would suggest a closer affinity to and understanding of each other's work.

Citizen's Advice Bureaux

Citizen's Advice Bureaux (CAB) were set up in 1939 at the outbreak of the Second World War to provide free advice to the general public, at a time when there was a rush of emergency legislation and administrative problems. Now there is a network of over a thousand local bureaux, dealing with millions of enquiries each year. The aims of the Citizen's Advice service are to ensure that individuals do not suffer through ignorance of their rights and responsibilities or of the services available, or through inability to express their needs sufficiently; and to exercise a responsible influence on the development of social policies and services, both locally and nationally.

The functions of the service are briefly to provide free and confidential advice and information, to refer enquirers elsewhere to specialist services, such as solicitors operating the Legal Aid Scheme, to act on behalf of clients by helping to complete forms, making telephone calls, writing letters or acting as an intermediary between the client and their adversary, seeking solutions acceptable to both sides, and providing feedback to central and local government through their day-to-day experience on matters of concern from individuals and the local community in general. Increasingly, Bureaux are becoming involved in debt counselling and in assistance to individuals facing tribunal appearances.

Bureaux are run by management committees comprising local community representatives. The daily organization of the Bureau is the responsibility of the Bureau manager who is usually the only salaried official. Other staff may be paid full time or part time, but more often than not the Bureau depends largely on the efforts of volunteers.

The National Association of Citizen's Advice Bureaux (NACAB) formulates national policy and coordinates the work of local Bureaux through a network of area committees. Citizen's Advice Scotland and the Northern Ireland Association provide similar services reflecting their different community needs. All Bureau staff are given training in the provision of community support services, counselling and interview techniques, prior to their first appointment. On-the-job training includes information retrieval, office routines, casework record-keeping and local media contacts. There are frequent refresher courses on new legislation, and specialist areas of work such as marriage breakdown, or housing problems. Citizen's Advice Bureaux are funded by local authorities, although they are an entirely independent organization. The National Association receives a grant from the Department of Trade and Industry, with similar grants going to the Scottish and Northern Ireland bodies.

A central information service prepares summaries of legislation and other essential facts, and provides a consultancy service for Bureau staff. A monthly information pack is sent to all Bureaux, and Citizen's Advice Notes Service (CANS) is generally available to all libraries and information bureaux. In classified form, it provides information on current legislation and administrative regulations affecting daily life and needs. It gives a concise statement of the current legal position on areas such as housing, education, employment and social services, and is kept up to date by regular supplements. The arrangement is in sections which are numbered within each section, making the detailed index at the front essential for proper use.

The Citizen's Advice Bureaux Service has developed in response to the need for professional advice and information which is independent and confidential, freely available to anyone in need, and usually delivered in the context of personal casework.

Information and advice centres

Many local authorities run information and advice centres as part of the policy of accountability to the local community, to promote better understanding of the council's role, and to act as an access point to local members of the council, and officers. These centres will provide information on all aspects of the council's business, such as planning applications, dates and times of meetings, councillors' surgeries, local leisure activities and problems with rents or payments of local taxes. Many information centres produce local free newspapers for general distribution, explaining council policies, providing advice and giving information on council services and problems. Some authorities prepare civic handbooks or guides for local industry or to attract potential employers, and these too are usually prepared by the local authority information or public relations departments.

In some urban areas with social problems, specifically targeted advice centres (for example on housing or legal problems) have been established. Sometimes funding for these is provided by the local authority, either in full or in part, or sometimes they are funded by the local community, and staffed by volunteers. They exist in response to particular needs, and they do much valuable work in fields where the established networks appear to be less effective.

Professional advice

Solicitors provide legal advice and represent their clients on a wide range of legal matters. Most of their work involves making wills and administering estates for probate, buying and selling property, preparing cases for court, and divorce and family problems.

Solicitors charge fees for their advice, and this can be very expensive, so many people pursue their legal affairs with the help of Legal Aid, which gives financial assistance towards legal expenses, depending on the person's financial standing. People who do not qualify for Legal Aid should be sure to obtain an estimate of the probable costs incurred before proceeding with legal advice and assistance.

Many solicitors are not in private practice, and some are employed by large organizations and corporate bodies. For instance, trade unions usually provide legal advice for their members, in the field of employment and industrial relations law, and the motoring organizations, such as the AA and RAC, advise their members on motoring or traffic problems, and provide legal assistance to pursue claims and to settle disputes.

Accountants give general financial advice on investments, taxation and mortgages. The Financial Services Act 1986 designates authorized financial advisers who must declare any interest in the financial products they recommend.

Bank managers also offer financial advice, but this usually concerns their own savings and investment accounts. Insurance brokers offer advice on insurance policies of all kinds, and on savings and pension provision.

Some advisers such as solicitors and accountants charge fees for their advice, whereas others may give free advice but earn commission on the financial products they sell. This may influence their advice, so it is always important to discuss this with an adviser before proceeding further.

The Consumers Association publishes many handbooks on consumer affairs, holidays, and financial services, with up-to-date reports in its monthly magazine *Which?*

Tourist information centres

There are over 700 tourist information centres in the United Kingdom giving help, and advice and information, to holiday-makers and users of leisure facilities. Most centres offer guidebooks, maps, books, holiday souvenirs and local craft goods for sale. They also provide leaflets on local holiday attractions free of charge. They supply advice on travel arrangements, including timetables for buses and trains, excursions and local features such as tide times. They also provide a comprehensive 'what's on' service for events and attractions such as theatre programmes and stately homes in the vicinity, with opening times and up-to-date prices.

Often tourist information centres provide a register of local accommodation and offer an on-the-spot booking service for visitors. This can be very difficult to organize, as the picture is constantly changing as each person is fixed up with their accommodation. In busy holiday resorts this can be a considerable undertaking requiring efficient systems and well-trained staff to sort out difficulties quickly to everyone's satisfaction.

Many of the independent information services are run with the cooperation and assistance of the public library service. Many Citizen's Advice Bureaux are housed in library buildings, and many libraries act as centres for tourist information. Often it is the need for specialist services beyond or outside the scope of the public library service which has initiated the establishment of these alternative sources of information and advice for the community.

Further reading

Citron, J., *Citizen's Advice Bureau*, Pluto Press, 1989.
Dossett, P., *Handbook of special librarianship and information management*, 6th rev. edn, ASLIB, 1992.
Library Association, *Industrial and commercial libraries*, LA, 1986.
Which? way to save and invest, 5th edn, Consumers Association, 1991.

4

Organizations and associations

Librarianship is a well organized profession in more ways than one. There are numerous associations and networks spread across the profession both in this country and abroad. Some are self-regulating, run by the profession itself rather than by employers or governments, and most are dedicated to spreading information amongst their members on matters of special or common interest.

This chapter examines several of the best known organizations, supplying information on their aims and purpose, their membership, the publications they produce, and the activities they encourage.

International organizations

The *United Nations Educational, Scientific and Cultural Organization (UNESCO)* has encouraged the development of public library services in Third World countries since 1945. It has done this by sponsoring projects, by arranging study visits for overseas librarians and by sending expert advisers overseas to act as consultants. Another important contribution has been the publications programme, which includes the quarterly *Unesco bulletin for libraries*, issued in several languages, a range of monographs on library topics, and the influential *Public library manifesto* which describes the basic services that public libraries should offer, with guidance on how they should be organized and financed.

The *British Council* aims to promote an understanding of British life and culture in other countries. As part of the programme the Council maintains more than 120 libraries in over 90 countries. It organizes exhibitions and exchanges, and sponsors visits by British experts to advise on numerous projects. It is particularly active in the field of teacher training and in English language teaching. The Council produces many publications on the arts, literature, business and industry in the United Kingdom, and is responsible for several publications of particular interest to librarians. *British book news* is a monthly survey of new British books, with reviews, bibliographical articles and a range of features and news about British books. *British medical bulletin* is a quarterly periodical which covers the latest research in a particular area of medicine, forming a valuable, up-to-date summary of the topic for doctors and medical research workers. The well-known *Writers and their works* series of pamphlets combines biographical information, critical appreciation and a short bibliography for each of the leading writers of English literature from Anglo-Saxon times to the present day.

The Ranfurly Library Service was established by the Countess of Ranfurly, in cooperation with the British Council and other international agencies, for distributing books to Third World countries where they are urgently needed. The service's Textbooks for Africa Project has succeeded in collecting over 350,000 textbooks which have been sent to over 20 African countries. Rotary International has cooperated generously with the Project by providing transport for delivering books, and contributions of money or books can be made by contacting the nearest Rotary Club.

The *Commonwealth Libraries Association (COMLA)* aims to develop links among Commonwealth countries in library activities, particularly with the education and training of librarians, visits and exchanges, with the establishment of Library Associations and with their development and support.

The *International Federation of Library Associations (IFLA)* pursues a similar role across a wider range of international library affairs, developing international cooperation in areas such as information sources and bibliographical standards of cataloguing practice.

The Library Association

The *Library Association* is the professional body for librarians and information workers in the United Kingdom. It was established in 1877, and its aims and responsibilities were set out in a Royal Charter granted in 1898. A supplementary charter was granted in 1986. Today the Association sets standards for the provision of services and professional conduct, represents the profession in discussions with central and local government and employing organizations, updates members of the profession by providing conferences, short courses, publications and information, maintains a register of chartered librarians, and oversees courses and qualifications in librarianship and information work. The Association also encourages high quality in book production and presentation by making prestigious awards each year, like the Carnegie and Kate Greenaway Medals, for children's books, to outstanding writers and illustrators.

Membership of the Association is open to all library and information workers in four categories: Personal members, including those preparing to obtain qualifications in librarianship; Associates who have fulfilled the requirements for registration as Chartered Librarians; Fellows, chartered members who have achieved the highest grade of membership; and Affiliated Members, who are library assistants and other paraprofessional staff. Affiliated membership was established in 1990. Such members can take part in professional activities, and enjoy the range of benefits that the Association offers to all its members except chartered status. They are subject to certain restrictions on voting rights. There is also provision for institutional membership for libraries and other interested organizations.

All members receive free membership of their Library Association Branch, organized on a geographical basis into the following regions:

Berkshire, Buckinghamshire and Oxfordshire
Eastern
East Midlands
London and Home Counties
Northern
Northern Ireland
North Western
Scottish Library Association
South Western
Welsh Library Association
West Midlands
Yorkshire and Humberside.

Branches organize meetings and seminars. All issue a newsletter, and some produce other documents and publications.

Membership of the Association also includes free membership of two Special Interest Groups. Additional Group membership is also available at a nominal charge. These Groups bring together staff working in a particular field or with a common interest in a special aspect of librarianship or information work. All Groups disseminate information about their activities, services and publications, usually by means of a regular newsletter posted to all members. The LA Special Interest Groups are as follows:

Association of Assistant
   Librarians
Audiovisual
Branch and Mobile Libraries
Cataloguing and Indexing
Colleges of F & HE
Community Services
Education Librarians
Government Libraries
Industrial
Information Services
Information Technology
International
Library History

Local Studies
Medical, Health and Welfare
   Libraries
Personnel Training and
   Education
Prison Libraries
Public Libraries
Publicity and Public
   Relations
Rare Books
School Libraries
University, College and
   Research
Youth Libraries

The Association of Assistant Librarians unites those members at an early stage in their careers. They have a very well developed publications programme, producing *The assistant librarian* each month, several basic texts aimed at newly qualified entrants to the profession, and important bibliographical works such as *Sequels* and *Fiction index*.

The Library Association has a permanent staff with a Chief Executive, who manages the work of the Association in three divisions: Education and International, Professional Practice and Management Services, with Library Association Publishing Ltd, which is owned by the Association. Policy is created by the LA Council which comprises Honorary Officers of the Association, and members elected in the following categories:

National Councillors

Councillors for National, University, College and Medical Libraries
Councillors for Special Libraries
Branch councillors
Group councillors
Affiliated Member Councillors
Association of Assistant Librarians Councillors.

Honorary Officers and committee members of Branches and Special Interest Groups are elected by the members in the Branches and Groups. Council meets regularly, and there are several committees and working parties to consider matters of professional interest or concern. The Association is also represented on several other organizations such as the British Standards Institution and the British Library, protecting the interests and presenting the views of members of the profession at every opportunity.

The Library Association provides advice and training on professional developments and recommended standards of provision by means of a comprehensive publications programme and by the Continuing Education Programme of short courses, meetings and seminars. The latest development is a framework for continuing professional development which gives all UK personal members the chance to update their skills and competences. Members also have access to the *British Library Information Sciences Service (BLISS)* which holds a comprehensive collection of books, pamphlets and periodicals, and operates a postal enquiry service. Online searching facilities are available through BLAISE-LINE. BLISS will eventually be housed in the British Library building at St Pancras which is now under construction.

Library Association Publishing has become probably the largest publisher of material on librarianship and information service in the world, with over 200 titles currently available, including well known titles such as *Walford's guide to reference material*, the *Library Association yearbook* and many important bibliographies. Several abstracting and indexing services began under the auspices of the Association. For example, the *British humanities index*, *Current technology index*, *Applied social sciences index and abstracts* and *Library and information science abstracts* all became established with the Association but are now published by Bowker-Saur.

All members receive copies of the *Library Association record* each month, which features news and articles, reviews, correspondence, obituaries and official notices designed to keep members up to date with all current developments. *The vacancies supplement* is posted fortnightly to every UK member's home address and it has become the foremost publication in this country for employers to announce vacancies in library and information work.

The Association also runs an employment agency for librarians and information workers – marketed under the name Infomatch – which not only finds employment for members, but also advises employers on how to solve their information needs by recruiting the most appropriate staff.

Aslib, the Association for Information Management represents individuals and organizations working in information gathering and dissemination. There are three regional branches: Scotland, North of England and the Midlands. There are also several Special Interest Groups:

Audiovisual
Biosciences
Chemical
Computer
Economic and Business
Electronics
Engineering

Informatics
One-Man Bands
Planning, Environment and
    Transport
Social Sciences
Technical Translation

Aslib publishes a selection of periodicals, monographs and directories on all aspects of information management. Members receive copies of *Aslib proceedings*, which records the papers delivered at meetings and conferences, *Journal of documentation*, which covers in depth articles and critical reviews of research, development and professional activities, and *Aslib information*, containing news, comment, reviews and current information.

Aslib's *Handbook of special librarianship and information management* is now in its sixth edition, having proved to be an essential standard work recognized throughout the profession. The *Directory of information sources in the U.K.* lists over 5,500 organizations providing information on all subjects. This comprehensive and authoritative directory is arranged alphabetically by title, with a separate subject index. The quarterly *Index to theses with abstracts* is the only comprehensive list of theses presented for higher degrees at British universities, polytechnics and other degree-awarding institutions. It is also available on CD-ROM.

Aslib is very active in the field of professional development and training, and provides and organizes a varied programme of seminars, courses, conferences and meetings, held at the Aslib Training Centre or presented on-site for corporate clients. Aslib is also connected with a professional recruitment agency that selects and recommends appropriate specialist information workers for employers, provides consultants and specialists for short-term projects and locates translators and indexers. A comprehensive library and information service is provided for members.

BSI

The *British Standards Institution* aims to prepare and publish national standard specifications and codes of practice for products, services, definitions and testing to ensure the quality of goods and services for industrial and personal use. Some products which are manufactured to BS specifications may apply to be endorsed by the Institution's Kitemark, which has become a well known badge of quality.

Standards are produced by committees of users, manufacturers and other interested parties with special subject knowledge. BSI also represents the views of British manufacturers on European and international bodies working towards agreement on quality standards worldwide. The Institution's Technical Help for Exporters scheme advises British manufacturers on the technical, legal and safety aspects of selling their products overseas. They also run extensive testing facilities and laboratories.

The BSI library deals with standards enquiries on a large scale, and maintains a collection of foreign and international standards which can be accessed online. The BSI yearbook lists all British Standards and Codes of Practice, extending to more than 10,000 documents, arranged in numerical order, with a comprehensive index and a section showing how British and international standards correspond to each other. *BSI news* is issued monthly and contains up-to-date information on new and revised standards, amendments and reprints. It also gives notice of draft standards for public comment, as well as more general coverage of developments concerning standards, the Institution and its work.

Many standards of interest to libraries are available on topics such as reprography, microforms, proof-reading and bibliographical recording. BSI is the British agent for the publication of the *Universal Decimal Classification* (see Chapter 7). Most libraries contain a selection of British Standards, and some larger libraries hold maintained sets either in hard paper copy in their familiar navy blue binders, or on non-photocopiable microfiche, kept up to date by annual subscription. Full-text standards have recently become available in CD-ROM format, which enables more sophisticated searching and retrieval techniques to be used.

Educational associations

The *School Library Association* aims to promote the development of primary and secondary school libraries, by increasing the role of the school library in curriculum affairs, in training for school library work, in contributing to reports and research projects, and in advising on funding and resource matters. The SLA publishes a range of practical booklets and bibliographies, and a quarterly journal, *The school librarian*, which features articles and book reviews. There is a network of local Branches which meet regularly for seminars, displays and to hear speakers on topics of interest.

The *Learning Resources Development Group* provides for the information needs of staff working in post-16 education who have responsibility in the field of learning resources, staff development and resource management in sixth-form, tertiary, further education colleges and higher education institutions. The Group organizes courses and conferences, issues the *Learning resources journal* three times per annum, and occasional publications on relevant topics.

The *National Council for Educational Technology* is the foremost body for promoting the development of audiovisual and educational technology materials and services, and actively disseminates information and advice to those employed in education and training. The Council publishes the monthly *British journal of educational technology*, and an extensive list of monographs on all aspects of educational technology, including an excellent series of *Open learning guides* in eight volumes, offering advice to all those involved in developing open-learning activities, and the four-volume loose-leaf *NCET directory of information*, which is a useful compendium of new developments in information technology and multi-media learning resources for education and training.

The *Scottish Council for Educational Technology* also aims to develop educational technology services, but with a particular emphasis upon Scottish affairs and on film and similar media. This is promoted through the Scottish Film Council on behalf of the SCET.

Book Trust

The *Book Trust*, formerly known as the National Book League, exists to promote books and reading by holding lectures and exhibitions, and producing book lists on a variety of topics. Book Trust brings together all those interested in books to highlight areas of concern such as the provision of books in schools, or the decline of public library services.

The *Children's Book Foundation* is a branch of the Trust specially formed to offer information and advice on books for children. It does this by maintaining an exhibition of recently published children's books, a register of authors who are available for personal appearances at promotional events, and by organizing Children's Book Week nationally.

The Book Trust also sponsors and organizes a range of literary prizes to encourage writers and illustrators, including the annual *Booker Prize* which is the foremost British prize for fiction and which attracts a great deal of public and media attention. The Booker Prize is now worth £20,000 to the successful author, and usually ensures greatly enhanced sales for the winning novel.

Book Trust Scotland is specially interested in Scottish books and writers. It organizes a collection of Scottish children's books and publishes a directory of children's writers in Scotland. Book Trust Scotland sponsors the Kathleen Fidler Award for an unpublished children's novel, and participates in the Edinburgh Book Festival and other Scottish literary events.

The Trust provides enquirers with information and advice through its Book Information Service, and by publishing a range of booklets and pamphlets on books and writers, including *Read easy* which lists material suitable for people with special needs or learning difficulties.

Further reading

Aslib, *We have the answer*, information pack, 1992.

Henderson, G.P. *et al.*, *Directory of British associations*, 11th edn, CBD, 1992.

Library Association, *Welcome: an introduction to LA HQ services for new members*, 1990.

Sanderson, Caroline, 'A day in the life of the Book Trust', *Bookseller*, 4 October, 1991, 956–7.

5

Government and control

Most libraries are responsible to higher authorities. Overall responsibility usually lies with the governing body of an institution or a local authority. It is this higher authority which ultimately controls financial and staffing matters, without which no library can function adequately.

The Public Libraries and Museums Act of 1964 lays down the legal framework under which public libraries operate in England and Wales. Briefly, the Act places responsibility for public libraries on the then Department of Education and Science, although responsibility now lies with the Department for National Heritage. Two Library Advisory Councils were established to assist the minister responsible.

Local authorities serving a minimum population of 40,000 were designated as library authorities. This resulted after local government reorganization in 1974 in a mixture of counties, metropolitan districts and London boroughs becoming responsible for public libraries in England. In Wales, the counties are the main providers, with one or two district councils in the main centres of population. In Scotland, the approach was reversed, with the majority of providers being district councils with three regional councils being added. Local authorities have a statutory duty 'to provide a comprehensive and efficient library service for all' and the service must be freely available. The main theme of the legislation is that the public library service should reflect and respond to the needs of the local community.

Review of local government

The present system of local government in England comprises single authorities in London and metropolitan boroughs in the other major cities, with county and district councils elsewhere.

Local government has recently been the subject of a ministerial review by the Secretary of State for the Environment, and as a result changes in the way local government is organized are likely to occur.

It was proposed at first that the present system should be replaced by single-tier authorities across the country, abolishing county councils in the process. This has already been announced for Wales, where the mixture of county and district councils will be replaced by single-tier authorities. Arrangements in Scotland are still under review at the time of writing.

The abolition of county councils will cause great problems for delivering library services in rural areas, including the lack of specialized bookstock and depth of coverage, and the deterioration of reference and information services.

Further consultations are being held, and agreements based on the advantages which accrue from economies of scale may result in some county councils being retained in a single- or two-tier arrangement in certain parts of the country where this may be more appropriate for community or geographical reasons.

Library committees

Local authorities appoint committees to administer their responsibilities in certain ways. Library matters are usually delegated to a special library committee, although they may well share a committee with some other allied sphere of interest. The chairperson of such a committee will be its leader, and the library spokesperson in council who acts as intermediary between the librarian and other elected members, and his/her knowledge of fellow councillors, overall policy and work on other committees, will be extremely valuable. The chairperson controls discussion in committee and should be well versed in all library matters. The committee will decide all matters of policy and planning, and the librarian is responsible for carrying out the administrative functions which make policy a reality. The librarian will report to the committee on a regular basis such matters as staffing, finance and extension activities. This is the opportunity to promote the needs and potential of the service. The librarian cannot decide policy, but he/she can initiate ideas and suggest possible courses of action for the committee to consider.

The modern trend is towards much larger areas of committee responsibility. Some local authorities have adopted systems of corporate planning which involve the setting-up of several management divisions. Libraries are often included in divisions with leisure, recreation and other public amenities. An overall director is appointed to each division with assistant directors responsible for each area of interest. This results in many chief librarians holding second- or even third-tier appointments, and thus losing direct access to their committees. On the other hand, many librarians have been appointed to directorships with increased responsibilities over a wide range of activities. Senior library staff are also expected to play a significant role in the planning, development and reviewing of library and other services, so that a properly corporate approach to problems can be followed at all levels of the service.

In educational libraries, similar management structures are often encountered. There is usually a library committee to decide policy and to advise on library matters such as finance and staffing. In smaller libraries, such as schools, and in industrial libraries, government and control may be vested in one person, e.g. the headteacher, or research director, and this can lead to more effective control, depending on the persons involved. The problems encountered, however, are unlikely to be as complex or as formal as in local authority services.

Finance

Money plays a crucial role in the administration and development of libraries. The extent and the quality of the library service will depend largely on the finance available since it is this which determines the provision of buildings, staffing and book purchasing, and a great deal of time and effort goes into ensuring that the money available is properly used and recorded.

Public libraries are financed mainly from local and central government sources, the main sources of income being the Council Tax, central government loans and grants, and charges for services and accommodation.

In 1988, the Government issued a Green Paper on *Financing our public library service*. The main proposals for debate in this document were wider powers to charge for some services, the encouragement of joint ventures between the public and private sectors, and the contracting-out of some services. It was argued that by charging for some services that were free, and by adopting economic charges for others, public library income could be considerably increased. The Green Paper stimulated wide discussion at the time. The Government reaffirmed its commitment to a free basic library service, but considerable debate ensued concerning its definition.

Much of this controversy has been resolved with the introduction of the *Library Charges Regulations 1991*, which are now in force. These permit the levying of charges for those services not ordinarily provided, and continued current practices such as charging for reservations, and supplying catalogues and printed material. There are also charges for staff time for conducting literature searches, for example, but not for user education except for using computers.

Many libraries now participate in various forms of income generation, such as charging for services, video hire, publications, attendance at arts activities and events, by selling off withdrawn bookstock, or even by offering new books for sale in library bookshops.

Each year the librarian must present an estimate of the financial requirements for the next year. These annual estimates may be in two parts. The first relates to items of capital expenditure, which usually include major projects such as new buildings or building extensions, and the purchase of very expensive items such as motor vehicles or computer equipment. The second concerns the revenue expenditure which consists mainly of recurring items such as staff salaries, bookfund, gas and electricity, transport, repairs and maintenance, loan charges and consumable items. The revenue estimates therefore include all the day-to-day running expenses of the library, and the capital estimates include all the major, permanent, non-recurring costs.

The estimates are prepared by the librarian, with the help of finance officers from the finance division, and are submitted to the local authority's library committee for approval. They are then considered by the finance committee, and possibly by the personnel committee if there are staffing implications, before being approved by a meeting of the full council. When the estimates have been examined and approved in this way, they become the official limits of expenditure for the service for that year. It is then the duty of the librarian to ensure that expenditure is kept within the limits of the appropriate headings, and to administer the amounts allocated as wisely and effectively as possible. The administration of the budget may be subject to inspection by local authority and central government auditors.

In educational libraries similar estimates of expenditure are calculated and go forward for approval by the various committees concerned. University libraries estimate their requirements against the background of expenditure for the university as a whole. Other educational libraries prepare estimates, with the overall budget of the college or school very clearly in mind. Industrial and special libraries also work on an annual basis within the framework of the needs and requirements of their institutions.

Staffing

An efficient and busy library will depend considerably on the calibre of staff that are employed. Public libraries often have to cope with an increasing volume of work, in the form of larger numbers of new books and issues. Therefore, the work needs to be highly organized and consistent, involving many routine processes. Long opening hours with mealtime and evening service and staff interchanges emphasize the need for efficient, well trained staff, who are sympathetic to readers.

It is one of the chief librarian's duties to determine how the library shall be run, and to ensure that it is being run properly and efficiently. The first step is to review the whole of the library's operations to see what services are required, and how they can be provided. Then the number of staff needed to meet the requirements can be assessed. The librarian prepares a list of the number and kinds of posts needed, with their appropriate grades, duties and responsibilities. These are approved by the appropriate governing body and become the staff establishment of the library concerned. A structure or framework of posts is thus created with varying emphasis according to the relative size and importance of each area of the work.

There will be one chief librarian, who is mainly concerned with the direction and leadership of the service as a whole, and who will spend much time on committee work, reports, correspondence and other administrative duties. In large library systems there may be more than one deputy or assistant chief librarian to supervise the general running of the library and to deputize for the chief when necessary. Various senior assistant librarians will take charge of major sections of library services such as reference, children's, cataloguing and lending departments. There will be senior librarians in charge of services based on geographical areas in large public libraries, and each full-time branch library will have a qualified librarian in charge. In addition there will be several assistant librarians to support their senior colleagues, trainee librarians who are not yet fully qualified and up to 60% of established posts may be filled by library assistants, who perform most of the front-line tasks in contact with readers and with the physical provision of materials for the library shelves. A modern development has been the introduction of many community projects sponsored by the Government through the Training Education and Enterprise Directorate, TECs and LECs. These have included several employment initiatives aimed at specific problems or at providing opportunities for particular sectors of the workforce, such as school leavers or the long-term unemployed. These initiatives have proved to be an important addition to the staffing resources available to libraries and other organizations, and many valuable and useful projects have been undertaken as a result.

From time to time vacancies arise or new posts are created and need to be filled. Most vacant posts are advertised to allow all interested persons to apply, usually in writing. When all the applications have been received a short list of candidates is chosen, and these may be invited to attend for interview for final selection. Each new appointee should be given a job description which outlines their duties and responsibilities and indicates how this post fits into the staffing structure and overall working plan. Salaries and conditions of service are negotiated and agreed nationally in public libraries, with perhaps some local variations for evening and Saturday duties. Large libraries will try to keep staff informed of administrative and professional developments by regular staff meetings, newsletters and bulletins. Some libraries have properly constituted staff associations which meet for educational and social activities. In smaller libraries, daily routine tasks may not be so time-consuming and repetitive and this also offers a greater variety of work and experience. Most library duties still remain to be done, but the volume of such work decreases, making fewer specialist posts necessary.

Staff training

Staff training falls into several categories. Induction takes place soon after appointment and is usually concerned with basic, introductory information about the workplace, the employer, health and safety, absence, pay and leave arrangements, as well as domestic matters like where to hang your coat, lunchtimes and tea breaks.

In-service training is concerned with how to do the job. It is usually organized during work time and involves individual or small-group discussions and demonstrations, talks, visits and job rotation. Staff may be offered secondment from work to attend courses at local colleges, on a day-release or full-time basis. The LA, AAL, ASLIB and many other organizations run short courses, conferences and meetings for library staff to attend. Some authorities may support staff who wish to pursue some aspect of their own personal development, such as an Open University course, which may not be specifically employment related.

More emphasis is now being placed upon staff appraisal as part of the whole staff development programme. At regular intervals staff are assessed and interviewed so that training can be specifically targeted at weak points in the person's knowledge or experience, or where the organization needs particular skills or abilities.

Staff records will be kept so that managers will have adequate information and advice concerning individual members of staff. A personal file will probably include the job description, salary and post details, training information, appraisal records, details of experience and sections worked, health and sickness records, secondment approvals and references that have accompanied applications for other posts.

Modern employment practice is regulated by many varied pieces of legislation. There is a wide range of employment law, governing such matters as health and safety, redundancy and unfair dismissal, equal pay, trade union membership, race relations and sex discrimination, and so it is essential that professional advice is sought on personnel matters.

Organization

Most library activities fall into three or four categories which can easily be identified and which help to form a functional framework. Library administration involves most financial, staffing and building matters, in addition to planning and development programmes. It also includes the review and analysis of all procedures, and the clerical and administrative duties common to most libraries. Bibliographical work will consist of acquisitions, book processing, classification, cataloguing and perhaps binding. Readers' services will include the normal lending and reference work and may also cover library publications and interlibrary cooperation. Extension activities, exhibitions and publicity work may be prominent enough to form another section.

Public libraries

Most public library systems now serve wider areas and larger populations than before, and with the introduction of larger library services and corporate management techniques, administrative services have become increasingly complex and are often housed in central corporation offices away from the main libraries. Frequently, bibliographical services are housed in a library headquarters, which again may be central and separate, since little direct work with readers is undertaken here. Most municipal libraries will have a large central library, usually in the centre of town, with large bookstocks and several departments. There is always a lending library for adult readers, and usually a children's library also. There is a reference library and this is probably the most important reference collection in the district and the centre for all reference and information services, handling enquiries from the public, from branch libraries and from other sections of the service.

A large specialist local history library is usually part of the reference service, and sometimes commercial and/or technical libraries also exist. Some large city libraries adopt a subject-departmental approach and there may be specialist library collections for music, social sciences and the arts. Branch libraries serve their immediate locality. Full-time branches offer lending services for adults and children, with possibly a quick-reference collection of the most frequently used material. Part-time branches and mobile libraries offer a lending service on a more modest scale. Various services to special categories of readers may include visits to the housebound, hospitals, prisons and schools.

County libraries often have the problems of serving large areas, with relatively small populations, since the more densely populated areas are served by municipal libraries. The major disadvantage of large areas is that bookstocks become more thinly spread and depth of coverage becomes more difficult. Several methods can be used to improve the situation and these methods are reflected in some county library practices, which are not usually needed in towns. Often, many more copies of titles are purchased, and the allocation and recording of bookstocks may be more complex, especially if books are circulated from branch to branch, or exchange and mobile collections are frequently revised. There will be a greater reliance on communications, transport and postal services than in the towns, and because there may be no central library, reference services in particular may suffer from the lack of a large centrally held bookstock. Reference and information services are usually carried on from county library headquarters, in addition to book requests and interlibrary loans. Some county and large municipal libraries have adopted a regional framework, where branches and staff are grouped together, and bookstocks merged for wider and more specialized coverage. In some areas, certain administrative functions have been delegated to regions, to give local staff and residents more participation in the running and organization of library services.

Equal opportunities

Most public libraries and many other organizations promote a policy of equal opportunities in respect of the people they serve and employ. This is usually interpreted as a commitment not to discriminate against anyone on the grounds of ethnic origin, colour, religion, gender, disability or political or sexual orientation.

Most public libraries provide services and facilities for ethnic minority groups within the community, and there is much more awareness of the problems of access to and use of public buildings by disabled people in terms of wheelchair ramps, self-opening doors and toilet facilities, although there is still work to be done in connection with other aspects of access, for example flexible application of regulations, staff training, and special needs awareness. Library services for the housebound are a feature of most modern public library services, and libraries generally have a good record with regard to facilities for the partially sighted.

Under Section 11 of the 1966 Local Government Act, grants are given by the Home Office and by TECs and LECs to finance projects supporting provision for ethnic minorities. Several staff appointments have been made to promote access to library services and facilities, but many authorities find that the temporary nature of the projects, and the complicated application process, make it difficult to maintain progress in this area.

Manchester Central Library is a good example of equal opportunities provision, providing books, music tapes, videos, newspapers, magazines, information sources, bilingual story books for children, and specialist staff in its Chinese Library serving the local Chinese community; and its Jewish Library with materials on Judaism and Jewish affairs in English, Hebrew and Yiddish. Manchester's Library Service for the Visually Impaired freely provides equipment for readers to use in the library, and links with other suppliers of materials for the partially sighted. The equipment includes Kurzweill reading machines, Viewscan and Optacon readers, microwriter word processors, manual braillers and specialist tape recorders. Full training in the use of these devices is available by appointment so that readers may visit the Central Library confident in the knowledge that specialist staff will be in attendance to see to their requirements.

In addition to the services offered most libraries are now very careful when selecting materials to ensure that they show a balanced view of everyday life, with common experiences that foster an understanding of cultural diversity and which avoid ethnic and sexual stereotypes. This is particularly important when selecting children's literature, so that attempts can be made at an early stage to remove barriers to the promotion of modern values in a multi-cultural society.

Education and special libraries

Most educational and industrial institutions prefer centrally situated library services. However, the larger universities and polytechnics may be located on more than one site, and if so, library facilities will also be dispersed, although administrative and technical services will be centralized. Many site libraries offer reader services in a particular faculty or subject area. Large industrial firms may also have libraries associated with the work of their various divisions. In the smaller libraries, work is varied since all aspects of library services are encountered. Staffs of two or three undertake most library duties, and share a more varied role, specializing in closely defined subject areas.

Further reading

Brown, R., *Public library administration*, Bingley, 1979.

Corbett, E.V., *Fundamentals of library organization and administration*, LA, 1978.

Harrison, C. and Beenham, R., *The basics of librarianship*, 3rd edn, Bingley, 1990.

Library Association, *Guidelines for training in libraries*, 8 vols, LA, 1981–91.

Norton, R., *Charging for library and information services*, LA, 1988.

Prytherch, R.J., *Staff training in libraries*, Gower, 1986.

6

Acquisitions and stock records

Book selection is a professional activity which very few library assistants should be asked to undertake, but it is useful to understand what is involved in the process.

Most libraries will have a book selection policy which will be based on the perceived needs of the community which the library is serving, and the policy will be implemented in the context of current publishing output. So it is important for librarians to build a community profile which identifies groups of people with common needs in library terms, such as young mothers with children, housebound people, local industries, ethnic minority groups, schools, residential homes, geographical features and any other factors which might influence library provision. This community profile should be regularly reviewed and amended if necessary, for example if a new housing estate is developed.

Librarians keep up to date with recently published material by visiting bookshops and library suppliers, who often maintain exhibitions or displays of new books, and by scanning publishers' lists, catalogues and announcements which are circulated regularly to libraries. Most librarians will read book reviews in the quality press and in specialist review journals, and many librarians will keep abreast of the whole publishing field by checking a weekly list such as the *British national bibliography* or the *Bookseller*. Some large libraries have regular book selection meetings, where senior staff meet to discuss book selection, exchange views and inspect approval copies before ordering additional copies.

The Net Book Agreement

The Net Book Agreement allows publishers to fix the price at which new books may be sold to the general public. As a result, most books sold in the United Kingdom are the same price wherever they are bought, and buyers do not have to shop around seeking the biggest discount, as they do for many other commodities.

There are several exceptions to the Net Book Agreement agreed by publishers. Books offered for sale during the National Book Sale held annually each Spring are an obvious example, and remaindered books are sold off cheaply because of poor sales at their published prices.

As a result of the Net Book Agreement booksellers do not compete with each other on price, but on other factors such as the attractive layout of shops, the helpfulness of the staff, and longer opening hours. Some major bookselling chains are increasingly hampered by the inability to generate further business by discounting or price cutting, and there are moves by some entrepreneurs to get around the agreement in the interests of more competitive trading.

The Publishers Association grants licences to certain libraries enabling them to purchase books at a discount of 10% from nominated book suppliers in return for allowing public access to their libraries. Public access is defined as meaning 'that the ordinary books in the library of the institution concerned shall not be restricted to the use of students or members of such institutional libraries, but that under proper safeguards and throughout the usual hours of such libraries they shall be available without charge, for public use within the library building'. Most public libraries operate licences, and many academic libraries permit access to the general public for reference facilities only, and thus qualify for a licence. Certain non-net books can only be purchased at full price. These are often published overseas, or they may be school textbooks meant to be purchased as multiple copies in class sets.

Many observers think the Net Book Agreement is an example of good practice which should be retained because it enables a wide range of books to be published. It ensures the protection of small independent booksellers, many of whom would go out of business, thus restricting availability and choice even further. Many academic or special-interest books would only be published at greatly increased prices, making them much more likely not to be published at all.

Book ordering

Most library books are obtained by either purchase, exchange or gift. They are purchased mainly from booksellers and not directly from publishers, except in the case of certain specialized reference works. There are three main types of bookseller: first, the specialists who may cater for foreign books, or children's, or special subject material. Next there are the general bookshops known to the general public. Finally there are also the library suppliers who offer large collections specially for public and institutional libraries, and who do not sell to the public. Periodicals may be bought from local newsagents, or from library supply agents specializing in foreign and academic journals. Some periodicals may be obtained from societies and firms individually.

Most library books are bought on approval, which means that they may be returned if they are unsuitable. After the initial selection has been made, order cards are usually made with full details included. Missing details are found and others verified by checking in general bibliographies such as *Bookbank, British national bibliography* and publishers' catalogues. Details such as author, title, publisher, ISBN and price are very important, since they identify the book accurately and mistakes can lead to duplicate ordering. Uniformity of entries is also important in this respect, especially when checking for previous copies. When the order cards are complete they are first checked against the library catalogue to see whether they are in stock, and then in the order file to see whether other copies are either on order or in progress. The items to be ordered are allocated to booksellers, and orders are typed on official order forms, which are then signed and posted to booksellers. Some booksellers send out lists or cards to help with book selection and these can be marked for ordering and returned to the suppliers. Orders can also be placed by telephone, fax or by personal visits, but some authorities require such orders to be confirmed on official stationery. Order cards are now supplied with the name of the bookseller, date of order and order number and are filed in the order files, and the library budget records are amended to include the latest order. The whole operation should be done with consistency and speed. The longer it takes, the more omissions in checking will be likely, as orders flow through the system continuously, and also the temptation to short-circuit the procedure for urgent items becomes greater.

In many large educational and public libraries, online computer ordering systems are replacing the older, manual methods. Every book title has an International Standard Book Number (ISBN) in hardback and softback, and this is usually all that is required by the computer to locate the full details by searching the machine-readable catalogue (MARC) database. All the necessary checking is done automatically before the computer places the order with a bookseller similarly equipped with online facilities.

AV materials

Acquiring audiovisual or multi-media learning materials can be more difficult and time-consuming than for traditional library stock. It is difficult because the mechanisms or instruments of bibliographical control are not always available, or because they are fragmented or biased towards the trade rather than libraries. It is more time-consuming to deal with more producers and suppliers, because there are very few library suppliers of the full range of this kind of material, although public libraries with their general requirements for videos and music recordings are probably better served than many academic libraries. There are not many generally accepted business conventions operating in this field, and libraries often have to establish terms and conditions of trade with several suppliers, and to negotiate the best discounts available which may vary significantly.

Audiovisual and multi-media materials need to be previewed before purchase, and it is difficult to scan a video in the way that experienced librarians can quickly assess a book by reading the blurb, the contents page, scanning the text and dipping into the index.

Video and audio material should be checked for faults, and processed for issue with the appropriate stationery. Many libraries keep archival copies of computer software to preserve the integrity of cassettes or packages which may be corrupted in use.

Budget records

Records of financial transactions should be kept as simple as possible. The records are to ensure that funds are spent correctly and that the budget is not overspent. It is also helpful in planning expenditure systematically, so as to ensure an even flow of acquisitions.

Each order and each invoice should be recorded separately so that it can easily be seen how much has been allocated for orders, and how much remains, and more importantly how much expense has actually been incurred on invoices. Many items which are ordered will never be received for various reasons and the invoices passed are the only true record of what has been spent. Unfortunately invoices usually lag too far behind orders to be reliable records themselves. Orders and invoices should be frequently compared, remembering that one represents estimated expenditure and the other actual.

Financial records should be kept in a way which ensures accuracy. Many libraries keep running totals of expenditure and remainders which confirm totals when added. Many devise other systems which cross-check similarly and thus eliminate errors. Large authorities keep their accounts by computer. Quite sophisticated financial information systems can sometimes be devised, if required, by analysing the accounts according to various factors, e.g. amounts spent per branch library in a large system, or by bookseller, subject or departments, or physical form – periodicals, audiovisual, books. This is one of the benefits of automated accounting procedures.

Exchanges and gifts

Often material may be acquired by exchange through Booknet, a service organized by the British Library. Libraries which benefit from the service are expected to offer similar free publications in return. Gifts of books and journals can often be quite fortuitous. Several bodies produce free material which can be supplied on request. Often this can be a valuable source of information not easily obtained in other ways. Material available from banks and building societies, voluntary organizations, company reports, careers and tourist literature, DSS and local authority information, are all important sources for the local community, and although much of it may be ephemeral it may have a topical importance that needs regular revision. Free material is only worth the trouble if it is appropriate to the needs of the library. Otherwise it becomes just as expensive as purchased items, in terms of clerical work, cataloguing, classification and shelf space.

Receipt

When books are received they are unpacked and checked against the delivery or advice note to ensure that the parcel contains what it is supposed to contain. The books are then checked against the invoice, which describes the goods despatched and states the amount charged. This entails making sure that the prices and quantities are as stated. Some libraries collate books at this stage, but many do not check the physical make-up of books at all, choosing to let imperfections show themselves in due course.

The goods received are then checked against the order to ensure that what has been delivered was in fact ordered in the correct quantities and formats. The order cards are located, and the date received and invoice number recorded. If a separate progress file is kept, the cards are moved there, from the order file. Invoices are passed for payment and budget records updated.

Processing

The books are then allocated to branches, classified, catalogued and prepared for the shelves. Most books are encased in plastic jackets. Date labels are attached and any necessary charging stationery, depending on the type of charging system in use. Spines are numbered with the classification number, and any other local processing is done, such as fitting security triggers. For a nominal fee, many booksellers will supply books ready prepared with jackets and the appropriate stationery to suit the requirements of most libraries. Books are then checked with their catalogue entries, preferably by staff from another section, and then displayed or shelved. Some items may be noted for inclusion in book lists or recent additions lists.

Periodicals

The acquisition of periodicals is similar to the procedure for books, but as they are received at regular intervals, they require special recording. Before ordering, details are verified in guides and bibliographies, and checked against current holdings and orders. Suppliers are chosen, orders sent and budget records altered accordingly.

On receipt of the first issue of a new journal, the item is checked against the invoice and its corresponding order. The invoice is then passed for payment, in advance of the receipt of the remainder of the year's supply. A record is kept of the order number, date, supplier and invoice details. Each succeeding issue is noted by recording the number of the issue and the date received in columns corresponding to the date of the issue. Many libraries house their periodical receipt records in horizontal index trays, and use coloured markers against a calendar scale to indicate at a glance whether copies are being received on time.

Omissions must be checked regularly and followed up promptly. Usually a telephone call will act as a preliminary reminder, but a letter or pro forma enquiry will probably be useful. A great deal of time can be spent chasing up late copies, or obtaining credit for non-arrivals.

Modern microcomputer software packages are now available for controlling the receipt and circulation of periodicals. Often these systems are able to print out overdue progress chasing letters, and keep budgetary and payment records.

The British Library Document Supply Centre offers a Journal Contents Page Service, which provides photocopies of the contents pages of any serials taken by BLDSC at a very reasonable cost on a subscription basis, so that only those journal articles which are of interest need be requested for loan, rather than subscribing to whole journals, where their interest is marginal.

Statistics

All organizations need standards to measure performance, achievement and efficiency. Statistics provide information to assist management decision-making, particularly when changes of systems are being considered. There are many problems in assessing and controlling a cultural or educational service. When using comparisons it is difficult to compare like with like. A good measure of performance is to compare current figures with last year's figures. This should show as accurate a picture as possible, if all variables are taken into account, e.g. population shifts. The following statistics are usually kept in libraries:

- Number of books purchased
- Number of titles purchased
- Number of books discarded
- Number of books in stock
- Population served
- Number of issues, per service point
- Number of interlibrary loans, reservations
- Number of BL applications
- Numbers of types of material, periodical, records, photocopies
- Daily issues, reference enquiries.

Figures on size of bookstock can be compared with national output, average prices and subject breakdowns and the unit cost of operations or transactions can be calculated, sometimes providing illuminating insights into the cost of various aspects of the service, which could pinpoint problem areas for improvement or investigation. Many of these figures fail to take quality into account, and they must be seen in the light of the library's policy and programme of objectives.

It is important for libraries to be able to measure their performance so that accurate assessments of their improvement or otherwise can be made, and the appropriate action taken to maintain the quality of their services, and to remain responsive to the needs of their users in terms of the materials available and the services offered. Accuracy in recording figures is essential, and any system with cross-checks will ensure accuracy. Running totals are also extremely helpful when information is needed urgently.

Stocktaking

Stocktaking is the physical checking of each book in stock. It is quite a simple exercise where the library is on closed access and some libraries that stocktake close until the operation is complete. Methods of stocktaking vary according to the kind of stock records in use. If an accessions register or a shelf-list exists, then each is useful, especially if recorded on cards. Cards are checked against the shelves, the issue, the stock, binding, repairs and other collections of materials in progress. The cards are marked to indicate the presence of a book at stocktaking. Cards for missing books are separated, re-checked at a later date, and withdrawn or replaced. This is probably the simplest way, but large systems can be more complex and the speed of the operation is essential. If the procedures extend over a period of days, the system that is being checked is changing as it is checked, and the results become more and more unreliable. Some libraries with automated issue systems and integrated catalogues may stocktake by reading barcodes on bookstock and printing out lists of missing books.

Many libraries no longer stocktake each year. Some undertake the operation at longer intervals, or as a random exercise. A continuous stocktake can sometimes be tried, through working slowly through stock records as other work permits, although the results may be unsatisfactory. Some librarians doubt the value of stocktaking, since it is a negative exercise which produces nothing. Gaps in stock can be found and covered through requests and reserves, and careful stock revision can eliminate most deficiencies. Missing books are indicated, but the losses cannot be stopped, or the books recovered. It is extremely costly in terms of staff time and completely disrupts the library's work while it lasts.

Stock records

The accession register is a record of books added to a library. Books are numbered progressively as they are added to stock and entered in the register, which may be in book form or on cards. There is no single method of compilation in general use, and many libraries have abolished accessions registers altogether. Details recorded include accession number, price, bookseller, date of addition, binding and discard, as well as the usual author, title and publisher. The accession number links the book with the bookseller's invoice and identifies each copy in the catalogue and the issue system. This link between the book and the invoice may also be useful for audit purposes.

A shelf-list is a stock record, in classified order, of bookstock at each service point. It may provide a link between the catalogue and the charging system when accession numbers are used for charging. Many libraries do without a shelf-list, preferring to rely on the classified catalogue instead.

The main stock record of any library is its catalogues, which are the keys to the library stock, arranged in a recognized order. Various added entries are included to ease tracing by different approaches. The catalogue records, describes and indexes the resources of a library.

Further reading

Chapman, E., *Buying books for libraries*, Bingley, 1988.

Feeney, M., *Net Book Agreement: to break or not to break, that is the question*, LA, 1989.

Ritchie, S., *Modern library practice*, Elm, 1982.

Spiller, D., *Book selection*, 5th rev. edn, Bingley, 1991.

Chapter 7

Classification and cataloguing

Classification gathers similar things together, and separates unlike things. Examples of classification are met every day in all kinds of circumstances and books are no exception. There are various classified arrangements for books, depending on different features. Most books are read because of their subject matter, irrespective of their publisher, title or even author, and so a subject arrangement is most useful to readers.

Classification in libraries has several advantages. It arranges books in a helpful order on the shelves, and assists in re-shelving books more easily. It refers quickly from the catalogue to the shelves, and offers a method of clear and effective shelf guiding. Issues and statistics are often recorded on the basis of the classification scheme in use, and special tasks such as stocktaking are often helped by the classification system. All in all it is a great time-saver, and assists in many routine library operations.

It is impossible to arrange subjects so that every relationship can be shown, and detailed subdivision often separates material which might be more usefully shelved together. Several disadvantages such as the changing order of knowledge, and the content and make-up of books, can seriously affect the usefulness of library classification. Problems such as the unavoidable disorder of bookshelves and the impracticability of reclassifying large sections of the library also impair its effectiveness.

Book classification

There are several special features of a book classification scheme which attempt to assist with problems particular to books. A *generalia* class includes books covering many topics, such as encyclopaedias, and may also include books whose interest lies in their form rather than in their subject content, such as collections and general periodicals. Many classification schemes use a generalia class to tidy up those items which do not easily fit elsewhere. *Form* classes are for books whose main interest lies in the form in which they are written, rather than in the topics which they may be about. Literature is such a class, where, for instance, a play or a poem about coal-mining will be read because it is a play or a poem, and very seldom because it is about coal-mining. *Form divisions* indicate a special way in which a book is written, or an aspect from which a topic is studied. Often, these aspects, such as history, apply to many subjects and common form divisions may be used to describe any topic.

The *notation* is the series of symbols representing the terms of the classification scheme. These symbols provide a convenient shortened reference to the actual class names. The symbols are added to the backs of books to help shelving, and provide a useful link between the catalogue and the shelves. The notation is essential for the practical application of a book classification scheme, and offers many practical advantages. It is used as a short sign on all parts of the book and in the issue system. It is a guide to the sequence of the classification tables, and enables use of the index to be made. Clear and efficient guiding of the shelves is made easier, and the efficient use of the catalogue is also helped. The notation may consist of any symbols, letters, figures or arbitrary signs and is said to be 'mixed' when two or more kinds of symbols are used. Notation may also increase the *mnemonic* value of a classification scheme. Mnemonics are memory aids which are frequently used to indicate certain aspects of a topic, which may be represented by the same symbols whenever they are used. Some classification schemes can indicate form divisions and geographical divisions in the same way each time they occur, and this reduces the need for repetition in the schedules. Mnemonics assist the memory by minimizing reference to the main tables, and are therefore a valuable, but subsidiary, quality of good notation.

For ease of reference, most classification schemes have an *index*, which comprises an alphabetical list of terms, with their corresponding notations. A good index should include all synonyms, and should help to ensure that topics are always classified in the same place. It also assists in finding subjects in the main schedules of the classification scheme, and on the library shelves. Many libraries use the index to a classification scheme as a substitute for a specially compiled subject index of the books in their collection. A *relative index* shows the relation of each subject to other aspects and subjects, so that alternative ways of treating subjects are not overlooked. The notation is provided for each subsidiary heading in a relative index.

Decimal Classification

The commonest classification scheme is the *Decimal Classification*, devised by an American, Melvil Dewey, in 1876 and now in its 20th edition. Because it is American in origin, and also because its original structure and general principles were formulated many years ago, it has some disadvantages for British libraries but is easily modified to suit local needs and is very popular, especially amongst public libraries.

The whole of knowledge is divided into nine subject areas, and a generalia class is also added. The ten main classes are:

001–099 Generalities
100–199 Philosophy
200–299 Religion
300–399 Social sciences
400–499 Language
500–599 Pure sciences
600–699 Technology
700–799 The arts
800–899 Literature
900–999 Geography and history

Each main class has ten divisions, each division has ten subdivisions, and so on. Subjects with more than ten subdivisions usually have minor topics grouped together at number nine as 'Others'. Throughout the schedules, practical usefulness has been given prior consideration over theory, and this has helped to make the scheme so popular.

Many critics complain of the illogical arrangement of classes and subdivisions, and of the artificiality of many divisions. Average classification numbers tend to be long, and the Western and in particular the American bias and terminology can cause problems. The scheme is of little value in special libraries but a shortened edition especially adapted for school libraries has been prepared. On the credit side it is relatively simple, easily understood, used and remembered. It is flexible and easily modified. It can be applied to material of all kinds, and is available in convenient printed form. An international organization ensuring its regular revision has been established for several years now. So many libraries use it that it has become almost the universal public library scheme. Its adoption by the *British national bibliography*, and its easy assimilation into computerized systems, has ensured its place as the most widely used scheme, despite the drawbacks it may have.

Other classification schemes

The *Universal Decimal Classification* (UDC) is a very detailed classification scheme often used in special libraries. It is based on Dewey's Decimal Classification and retains this order and character in outline, although it has developed separately and there are now many other differences. There is no three-figure minimum notation, so that main subjects can be represented by one or two digits only (e.g. Applied Science 6, Engineering 62). Where there are larger numbers, decimal points are used to divide at three-digit intervals (e.g. Radar 621.396.96). Several arbitrary signs (e.g. + / :) are introduced to indicate relationships, and there are tables of special subdivisions to indicate form, place, time, language and other aspects. This mixture of signs, numbers and sometimes letters can give very detailed and complex placings, but the notation may become quite cumbersome. UDC is published and kept up to date by the British Standards Institution, in Britain, and one advantage is that Dewey's American bias is therefore not reflected in the terminology or structure.

The *Colon Classification*, first published in 1933, was devised by Dr S. Ranganathan and adopted a new approach to library classification. The scheme is not a list of subjects or topics in a pre-arranged order, but instead it enables class numbers to be constructed by adding components from different schedules, using arbitrary signs as links and indicators. Ranganathan claimed that a suitable classification number could be built up in this way for any topic, however complex. The *Colon Classification* is not used in a large public library, but its theories have had widespread influence on many special subject schemes such as the *London Education Classification* and the *sfb Construction Industry Classification*.

The *Library of Congress Classification* began as a special scheme to meet the particular requirements of the Library of Congress, which houses a vast collection with many special problems. The classification was not devised with any particular theory in mind, but rather with the contents of the Library and the patterns of usage foremost. This arrangement of grouping according to the ways in which the literature of a subject tends to be structured and used by writers and scholars is sometimes called 'literary warrant'. In practice, each main subject is completely separate, with an individual framework and its own index. The main classes and subdivisions use an alphabetical notation, and further subdivisions are numerical. This gives a lengthy, mixed notation which can be difficult to remember and use. There is no general index. The scheme is effective and generally works well and although it is obviously very popular in the United States it is not widely used in British public libraries, although some university libraries use it. The schedules are revised promptly, and uniformity is ensured by the use of printed cards and machine-readable catalogue (MARC) tapes produced by the Cooperative Cataloguing Division at the Library of Congress.

The *Bibliographic Classification* was first published by Bliss in 1935, and a second revised edition has been appearing in parts since 1977. It is arranged in a scholarly and logical way generally accepted by academics as being the way in which subjects are taught and practised. Subjects are developed from the general to the particular, and related subjects like science and technology are arranged together. There is provision for alternative placings, but this adaptability can also be confusing and lead to inconsistencies. Auxiliary tables are provided for compound subjects, and spaces are left for new subjects to be inserted. The notation is mainly alphabetical. There are simple form divisions and a good relative index.

Practical classification

Broad classification is a term used to indicate the use of the main sections of a classification scheme to minimize the complexity for readers. It may be introduced in a small library or, especially, in a children's library. It offers the advantage of shorter classification numbers which can also be expanded as the collection grows.

In many libraries, novels and light fiction are taken out of Dewey sequence and are filed alphabetically by authors' surnames. Often quick-reference books are shelved in a convenient, separate sequence. Music scores and other categories of special material such as oversize books may also be shelved on the bottom shelf of each appropriate tier, or in a separate sequence altogether. These provisions for oversize books are known as *parallel arrangements*, and any alteration of the normal sequence of books, for example by shelving language and literature together in Dewey, is called *broken order*. Any variation in the general shelving pattern should be indicated to the reader via the catalogue.

Catalogues

A library catalogue is a list of books and other material available in that library, with entries arranged in a recognized order, containing information about each book or other item. It gives the reader an overall view of the entire bookstock, or those sections of it which are required. It is the key to the whole stock of a library, a locating device and an indispensable staff tool.

Most British libraries construct *classified catalogues* in which entries are arranged by their subject classification numbers, so that entries for books on the same subject will be found together and will be beside entries on related topics. Because the main catalogue is in subject number order, two indexes are needed to help readers to locate the items they require.

The *subject index* is an alphabetical index of subjects showing the classification numbers assigned to each subject. The *author index* has entries arranged in alphabetical order of authors' surnames. To find out what books the library has on any subject, the reader must first consult the subject index to find the classification number for that subject. Then the reader must consult the classification number in the catalogue or go straight to the shelves to see what is immediately available on that topic. To find out if the library has a book by a certain author, the reader should consult the author index, and this again will refer the reader to the classified catalogue, if additional details are required.

A *dictionary catalogue* lists entries under headings arranged in alphabetical sequence. Specific subject headings are chosen, and the reader is directed from one subject to another by an elaborate system of 'see' and 'see also' references. Some dictionary catalogues have separate author and subject sequences, but most are filed together alphabetically. The range of material that a library holds is not immediately apparent, since related topics are filed by the accident of their alphabetic titles, but many readers seem more familiar with alphabetic arrangement, which can also show titles in addition to subjects.

Cataloguing rules

Whichever type of catalogue is used, each book will have a main entry which lists the book under the name of the author, or body responsible for its creation, together with full bibliographical details (see Figure 1). There is only one main entry, but there may be many added entries for joint authors and other subordinates, e.g. editors, translators, series.

The main entry is usually divided into five parts, namely:

1 *Heading* – this is usually the name of the author or body responsible for producing the book.
2 *Title* – this is written as it appears on the title page. It includes the name of the author, or editor, and also the number of the edition, other than the first.
3 *Imprint* – this comprises the place of publication, the publisher and the date.
4 *Collation* – this is the physical description of the book, including the number of volumes, pages, illustrations, size and series, if any.
5 *Notes* – these are bibliographic notes concerning, for example, the publishing history of the book and should not be confused with the annotation which refers to the contents of the book, or its intended readership.

Rules are laid down to ensure accuracy and consistency when cataloguing. Committees of librarians in North America and the United Kingdom have collected together a cataloguing code of rules which are generally agreed to be the best way of preparing catalogue records in the majority of libraries. This cataloguing

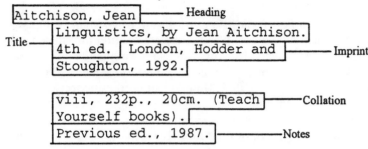

Figure 1   The five parts of a catalogue main entry

code is called the *Anglo-American cataloguing rules,* and was first published in 1967, superseding a much earlier code of 1908 which gave British and American alternative versions for several problems.

A second edition of the *Anglo-American cataloguing rules* appeared in 1978, which was widely referred to as *AACR2,* and a revised version of the second edition became available in 1988. This latest revision continues to follow the principles and underlying objectives already agreed in earlier editions, and extends the coverage to include consideration of computerized cataloguing, the increase in centralized and cooperative cataloguing, and the newer types of audiovisual and other library materials. The rules are intended to give guidance on a comprehensive range of possible headings and entries, and as such provide a detailed and complex set of examples, which are extremely valuable to practising cataloguers.

Physical forms of catalogue

Library catalogues were once frequently produced in *printed book* form. This is the quickest and easiest form of catalogue to consult, but it is uneconomic to produce, and soon becomes out of date. Entries cannot easily be added, and there is very little flexibility. Printed catalogues were quite popular when library bookstocks were more static, or perhaps organized on closed access, and there are still some fine examples produced for special collections.

The *guard book* was compiled on the scrapbook principle. The flexibility of the printed catalogue was improved by leaving spaces or inserting extra pages when required. Although this was a partial solution, maintenance was still difficult, and additional copies were needed while the others were updated.

Sheaf catalogues carry separate paper entries in loose-leaf binders, which can be taken to the shelves, when consulted. Unfortunately they can also be lost. They offer complete flexibility, but are slow to use. They can be stored in a variety of ways, since they can be brought to reading height when in use. Entries can be duplicated by typewriter using carbons.

Card entries are filed in drawers, stored in cabinets. These are simple to maintain, but take up considerable space, since they must remain at reading height and can only expand sideways. Readers often complain about congestion at card cabinets, since one user effectively prevents another from using all the immediately adjacent catalogue drawers. Solutions to this have been tried by spacing drawers more widely, or by allowing access from the front or back simultaneously, but the problem remains largely unsolved.

The main problems arise from the dual use of catalogues. The librarian, especially the cataloguer, needs a flexible catalogue which can accommodate additions and withdrawals easily, at any time. Readers are primarily concerned with quick and easy consultation, regardless of whether someone else may be using it at the same time.

Where computer catalogues are used, they are often produced in microfilm form, either in cassettes or on microfiche. Although they are extremely efficient to produce and amend, they must be consulted by using microreaders. The problem of congestion among readers still remains, and some readers are reluctant to use them. One big advantage is that copies can be cheaply produced, giving small libraries access to the complete stock of larger library systems. Some are kept up to date by supplements, and these can prove wearisome to use, particularly if fully revised, updated versions are issued infrequently.

Some libraries have computer catalogues which enable readers to consult catalogue records by using computer terminals. These are known as *online public access catalogues (OPACs)*. These are often quite user-friendly, and members of the public find little difficulty in searching for specific items. In fact many people prefer to use online catalogues, and often this is because subject searches can be much more easily undertaken than with the more traditional catalogue formats. Many systems now allow readers to print out lists of items that have been found.

Some catalogues are integrated with issue systems, and this enables readers to inspect circulation records, and reserve materials for themselves. As computer systems become more user-friendly, and equipment becomes more readily and cheaply available, improvements and developments will become more widespread. It will be essential for readers to use OPACs quickly and easily and so adequate point-of-use instructions and simple on-screen directions will be of crucial importance, otherwise the complexities will just become a barrier to use. There must be sufficient terminals to avoid waiting time for readers, and to accommodate periods of downtime, when machines may be undergoing maintenance or repair.

Centralized cataloguing is carried out by a central library or organization so that all member libraries may share the cataloguing, thereby avoiding duplication of effort and providing a uniform standard entry. The British Library Bibliographic Services Division produces MARC computer tapes, which are a machine-readable version of the *BNB* and the Library of Congress bibliographic records. Subscribing libraries use the MARC tapes to produce local catalogues with their own computers, or a complete catalogue service can be provided to meet the requirements of individual libraries. Cooperative networks can be established to produce a central computer database which other libraries can also use. An obvious example of such a network is the Birmingham Libraries Cooperative Mechanization Project (BLCMP), which provides a cataloguing service for subscribing libraries, and has taken over the production of printed catalogue cards previously issued by the British National Bibliography. Since 1977 an online computer system known as BLAISE (British Library Automated Information Service) has facilitated general library housekeeping routines from cataloguing to bibliographic checking, and cooperates in the production of *Books in English*.

A *union catalogue* is the combined catalogue of the bookstocks of various libraries or branches. It makes the total book resources for an area available for consultation by everyone in that area, and provides book locations.

Catalogue filing

Before any filing is done, it is essential to discover which method of filing is used: whether it is the 'letter by letter', also known as the 'all through' method, or the 'word by word', sometimes called the 'nothing before something' method.

'Letter by letter' means that word formation on the card heading should be ignored. Each letter as it follows the next is considered for its place in the alphabet, and for no other reason. For 'word by word' filing, each word is taken as it appears, using the same strict letter order, but in this case stopping at the end of each word.

The following example, taken from a section of a subject index relating to books on all aspects of children, illustrates clearly just how much difference is made when one method is chosen rather than the other. It also shows the necessity of ensuring that one single method is followed consistently at all times, by every member of staff.

Letter by letter	*Word by word*
child allowances	child allowances
childbirth	child guidance
child guidance	child psychology
childhood diseases	child welfare
childkilling	childbirth
child psychology	childhood diseases
children in care	childkilling
children's games	children in care
children's literature	children's games
child welfare	children's literature

Withdrawal and disposal

Catalogues must be constantly revised to ensure accuracy and consistency. Much ephemeral material is best left uncatalogued and is therefore easier to discard, e.g. travel information and careers literature. Often where the relevance of material is uncertain, an intermediate step, such as relegation to a stack or reserve collection, can be introduced, provided that catalogue entries are suitably amended. New editions will almost certainly render older copies obsolete. These may be discarded or circulated to branch libraries where bookstocks may be less representative.

On withdrawal, all relevant records should be amended or discarded, as appropriate. Withdrawals should be notified to headquarters sections, for union catalogue amendments, and some items may be offered to subject specialist libraries. Some libraries offer older material to their readers for sale. Most discarded material is mutilated or destroyed to prevent unauthorized resale elsewhere. All discards should be clearly marked, statistics kept and stock records altered accordingly.

Further reading

Chapman, L., *How to catalogue*, 2nd edn, Bingley, 1989.

Hildreth, C., *The online catalogue*, LA, 1989.

Hunter, E.J., *Computerized cataloguing*, Bingley, 1985.

Hunter, E.J. and Bakewell, K.G.B., *Cataloguing*, 3rd edn, Bingley, 1991.

Online catalogues, Library Information Technology Centre, 1988 (LIBS, no. 7).

Rowley, J.E., *Organizing knowledge*, Gower, 1987.

8

Good housekeeping

One of the aims of staff working in any type of library should be to ensure that the right book or right information is produced as speedily as possible after a request has been received.

One of the main factors causing delay is the 'lost' book, which may have been sent for rebinding, withdrawn for repairs, put on one side because it is reserved or required for interlibrary loan; or may simply be missing through having been wrongly shelved.

Good housekeeping ensures that the incidence of lost and missing books is kept to a minimum. After a returned book has been discharged, it should be briefly inspected for any minor repair requirements, any recent damage and to see if the date label requires renewing. The observant assistant must also be on the lookout for any notes or signs which may indicate that a particular book should be retained at the counter because there is a waiting list for it, or because it has been requested on interlibrary loan.

Shelving

The first task is to sort the books into categories, e.g. fiction, non-fiction, oversize, out of sequence; the second task is to arrange each category of books into the exact order in which they will appear on their respective shelves. If possible it should be arranged so that the books can all be disposed of in one circular trip round the library. It is worth noting that efficient shelving is only achieved when the library assistant is thoroughly familiar with the shelf arrangement and with any 'exceptions to the rule' which might appertain in his or her own particular library, e.g. the language (400) and the literature (800) Dewey main classes are often located on adjacent shelves to suit the borrowers' convenience.

A new assistant would be well advised to spend some time coming to terms with the stock and its location before shelving. Sometimes before starting the actual shelving it may be necessary to rearrange the shelves, loosening books in order to insert further books with ease. Another point worth noting is that the appearance of books is neater if they are straightened so as to be level with the front edge of the shelves. By doing this, differences in book sizes become less obvious, and the resulting uniformity helps to maintain the tidy appearance of the library.

In addition to the routine shelving sessions, good housekeeping demands that books and other printed materials are sorted through at regular intervals and checked that they are in correct order. At the same time a check should be made on the visibility of the titles of works and of labels indicating classification numbers and so on, since with time the latter often become mutilated or illegible. Not only does regular renewal of labels help in the general good appearance of the library; it also helps to ensure that non-fiction books are shelved at their correct place in the classification scheme.

In the majority of libraries there are special categories to be noted, such as reference, pamphlet or oversized material, and usually each category has its own special symbol or code which is added to the catalogue entry.

Large libraries have often built up their own specialist collections, and because of their size, they too are often treated as out-of-sequence material, since they are housed separately from the main sequence, and duly indicated on the catalogue entry. Most types of libraries, including both public and special, tend to arrange displays of various kinds from time to time; thus stock is temporarily removed from its normal sequence on the shelves, and placed in the display area.

Storage of non-book materials

Non-book materials are yet further examples of items not housed in the normal book sequence. Too much direct heat, from radiators for example, causes items such as records to warp, whilst strong sunlight can play havoc with items made from paper, even to the extent of constituting a fire risk. The dust contained in the atmosphere and the humidity of a particular environment are factors to be taken into consideration before certain items are housed. Both open- and closed-access locations need to be carefully vetted for any possible damage to materials.

Some libraries carry a separate catalogue for each type of audiovisual material. But it is also necessary to draw the attention of borrowers to the different types of media available. Many libraries place examples of non-book materials in a prominent position on the wall or at the counter. Displayed record sleeves, for example, can indicate the existence of a library's record collection, and also have the additional effect of brightening up plain walls and dark corners.

Videos

Video recordings are usually stored securely in shallow filing cabinet drawers, and their empty boxes, with promotional material and short synopsis, displayed for public browsing.

CDs

These are similarly stored separately in cardboard envelopes, with their cases available for display and browsing.

Slides

Slides can now be housed in commercially produced slide boxes, each slide having its own individual slot. When preliminary viewing of slides is required, for a selection of slides to be made, it is essential that slides are stored in such a way that they can be easily inspected. In this case, slides are best housed in transparent plastic wallets, with a separate pocket for each slide. These wallets are then stored in suspension filing cabinets. By holding such a wallet in front of a light or a window, the user is then able to examine its contents without needing to handle each slide separately. Similar see-through wallets, though somewhat smaller and holding around 12 slides, can be placed in ring binders. The whole unit then resembles the form of a book, and can be shelved vertically like the bookstock.

Newspaper cuttings

The ways in which a library stores its newspaper cuttings are dictated by the purpose of its collections and also by the length of time for which they will be required. A collection of cuttings on a topical subject, which is likely to be quickly outdated and therefore discarded, can be housed in a box file. As each cutting is acquired the name of its source, i.e. that of the newspaper or magazine, along with its date are written at the top of the cutting which is then simply added to the existing contents.

Cuttings intended to form a more permanent collection are mounted on to thin cardboard of uniform size, supplied at the top with a uniform heading consisting of topic title, name of its source, and the date, and deposited in a filing cabinet. Here the cuttings will be arranged in the order considered most appropriate, which may be chronological or under different aspects of the topic.

Some cuttings collections lend themselves to being housed in a scrap-book, each cutting simply being pasted into the book on its arrival. Alternatively, if the collection is going to become a permanent item of library stock, the cutting can be kept loose until the total collection has been acquired, and then arranged systematically into the scrap-book. Pasting cuttings on to the single sheets of a loose-leaf binder is a useful way of ensuring the flexibility of a collection.

Maps and charts

The cheapest method undoubtedly is to have the map or chart rolled up, with one of its open ends visible, and either stacked on a shelf or fitted into a rack resembling an umbrella stand. The end of the map can have a tag dangling from it to indicate its subject matter. However, it is more satisfactory to provide a set of shallow drawers known as a *map chest*, which enables maps to be stored flat and consequently to be more easily used.

The most effective way of map and chart storage is achieved by some form of suspension since this enables the items to be examined instantaneously. There are sets of wall-mounted arms available which grip a set of maps or charts. These arms are pivoted so that the user is able to browse through the entire collection, and even detach one item if he wishes to examine it more closely on a flat surface. Alternatively, maps can be held by large bulldog clips, which can be threaded on to a rod so that the maps are suspended, making them easier to consult.

Good housekeeping

Whatever the storage method adopted by a particular library, constant care has to be taken to ensure a longer life for the inevitably fragile collections of maps and charts. Some libraries are now taking slide photographs of their charts, so that borrowers can examine the scope of the collection without the actual charts being handled. Libraries are beginning to invest in seal presses which facilitate the reinforcing of maps and charts by laminating and backing them with strong transparent film.

Microfilm

Each microfilm consists of a continuous roll of film and this is kept in a cardboard box. Upended, the cardboard boxes, each labelled with appropriate information such as title and supplier, are stored in sliding drawers within strong metal cabinets. Microfilm readers, which project a magnified image of the microfilm on to a screen, are made available in the library itself, so that the intending reader is able to locate and study for himself the particular item which interests him.

Microfiche

This is a type of microform which was commonly used for the presentation of a wide variety of information. Individual fiches can be fitted into sleeves and held in a hardbacked ring file like a book. Magazines and journals can be ordered in microfiche form, the whole of one issue of a journal appearing on a piece of microfiche roughly the size of a postcard. Each microfiche is placed in its own separate pocket-type envelope so that the heading of each is clearly visible. Yearly indexes to the articles contained in the journals, also in microfiche, are filed in their appropriate place, and all are housed in metal drawers/cabinets.

Computer software

Computer software is usually stored on floppy disks, and these items should be stored away from radiators and windows since direct heat or sunlight could corrupt the package. Since not all software runs on every type or model of computer, the software needs to be arranged according to the hardware required, so that users will not select incompatible programs.

Records

Ideally, record collections should be made available to be browsed over by the intending borrower. Library equipment manufacturers sell record browser boxes which will hold and support records in such a way that the front of the first record and then each subsequent one can be seen as they are moved forward. Some libraries, wanting to encourage browsing yet also wishing to prolong the life of their records, have only the commercial sleeve available in the browser box. The record itself is kept in closed access, housed in a plain cardboard sleeve on which is recorded the disc's identification and location.

In spite of all the precautions taken to preserve records, they are still amongst the most vulnerable items of a library's stock, not least when out on loan. Some libraries do not allow records to be lent until the stylus of the record player on which they are to be played has been brought to the library for inspection. More libraries, in particular the specialist ones with large record collections, are choosing to produce their own cassette tapes from their records, and to make these, rather than the records themselves, available for loan.

Since browsers' requirements in relation to records are usually most specific, much care and thought has to be given to the arrangement of records within a library's collection. It is usual to arrange classical music records in alphabetical order by composer. Non-classical music is divided into categories such as pop, jazz, progressive, brass and arranged in alphabetical order by artist; whilst spoken-word items are arranged alphabetically by author or artist as appropriate.

Guiding

Libraries can be confusing places. Next time you visit a large department store compare how easily you find your way around the merchandise on offer, to how difficult it can be to locate the section you require in a library, with its seemingly strange numerical system of arrangement! Libraries generally do not give as much emphasis to good layout, appearance and design. Many issue *printed guides* with floor plans and detailed explanations on how to find a book, using the catalogues and classification scheme. Some have large diagrams on public view, and some have colour-coded directional signs. There should always be staff available to give assistance and to point the reader in the right direction.

Most, however, rely on shelf guiding to supply their readers' requirements. The term 'shelf guiding' covers a wide variety of types of printed headings. These range from the very general, which aid in the locating of the broad categories of books, to the very specific, which, attached to the edge of a shelf, indicate the contents of that particular shelf or part of the shelf. Whatever techniques are used in the making of headings, it is helpful if the library assistant, who inevitably makes frequent and regular journeys round the shelves, can quickly spot any deterioration in the condition of the guiding, and put any necessary repairs into operation.

A good printed library guide should contain most of the following types of information: how to join and who is eligible, how to use the catalogue and classification scheme, procedure for borrowing reservations and interlending, essential rules, regulations and charges, specialist services such as archives or play sets, photocopying, the layout of the library, opening hours, address and telephone numbers including those for other branches or departments, and an invitation to approach the staff for assistance.

A reader's adviser should always be in attendance to provide personal contact, to help and recommend, and to deal promptly with requests and reserves. They should be accessible and outgoing with good interpersonal skills, well versed in current affairs, knowledgeable about current publishing output; and aware of the facilities offered by other departments and libraries. Due to shortages of staff many libraries cannot give this individual attention, or maintain the range of bibliographical material needed for the best possible service. Smaller libraries have closer relationships with their users, but often there may be insufficient staff to give an effective service to readers in this way.

Book display

Nothing enhances the neat, orderly appearance of a well organized library more than colourful eye-catching displays of books and other materials. These can help to break the monotony induced by rectangular shelf units, furniture and books alike, especially if the displays are framed by tastefully arranged plants, dried flower arrangements or ceramics. It is not necessary to have great artistic talents at one's disposal in order to mount a display. The aim is to choose a topical or otherwise appropriate theme, and to express that theme in such an original way that the reader's attention is caught.

In addition to books and other printed material a good display can be augmented by such items as photographs, cuttings, charts and models. Approaches to the art and craft departments of schools and colleges and to a group such as a local photographic society, can result in excellent items being offered on loan for display purposes. Posters advertised in the press can be obtained, and much useful and colourful background material acquired from travel agents or foreign embassies. Free material such as trade handouts can also serve as an invaluable aid in display work.

One of the purposes of displaying a selection of non-fiction is to draw the borrower's attention to books allied to his own subject, which are placed in different sections of the library's classification system. The lettering used for display work and posters should always be simple, so as to be eye-catching from a distance. Proficiency in the use of one or more of the many types of lettering kits now available can save both time and the unnecessary effort involved in producing free-hand lettering. Many libraries now use desktop publishing or word processing facilities for effective displays which can be easily designed and produced.

Finally displays should never be allowed to look 'tatty' or neglected. They need to be changed frequently and regularly if their purpose is to be achieved. Before the next change of display takes place, however, it is important to list all the books used to illustrate the theme. These can be stored in a folder along with any other display material thought worth keeping to form the basis of any similar display in the future.

A library's appearance can make or mar a borrower's pleasure in his surroundings. The good housekeeping aspect of librarianship is one in which the library assistant has a vital role to play.

Minor repairs

Repairing minor damage to books is also a part of good housekeeping. A variety of repair material is available and an interested worker can find satisfaction in developing skills appropriate to the task in hand. There are a number of branded transparent tapes which can be used for torn pages, maps and documents. The majority of these do not colour or contract with age; they are therefore quite permanent, and can be written on, using pen or pencil. Coloured tape is available for the edge binding of book covers, maps and pictures, for extra protection, and these tapes can be applied with the aid of an edging machine. Adhesive waterproof tape of varying widths for protecting and reinforcing the spines of books can also be bought, and plastic wallets are available for protecting paperbacked books.

Binding

There are several commercial firms who specialize in binding and conservation of books and other library materials. Hardback library books can be rebound and strengthened quite cheaply to lengthen their life and to look like new books again. Journal and reference book binding is also considered by many libraries to be an appropriate form of protection and storage. Paperback reinforcing is another way of prolonging the shelf life of this type of material cheaply. Special categories of binding such as theses, antiquarian and fine binding are also undertaken, as are special conservation techniques and processes for archive material.

Journals are bound to strengthen and protect them from physical damage, and to give convenient access to individual issues, often through indexes which are bound into each volume. Broadly speaking, books are re-bound to save money by prolonging the life of well used volumes, and also to keep others in circulation which can no longer be replaced.

Further reading

Carey, R.J.P., *Library guiding*, Bingley, 1974.
Fothergill, R. and Butchart, I., *Non-book materials in libraries*, 3rd rev.edn, Bingley, 1990.
Prytherch, R., *The basics of readers' advisory work*, Bingley, 1988.

9

Lending procedures

Reader registration

Many libraries keep a record of those persons who are entitled to use the library, so that they can be easily identified.

In public libraries a readers' register is usually compiled by filing membership application cards. Potential readers are asked to complete a form giving personal details, and which usually contains an undertaking to comply with the rules of that library. The reader's eligibility for membership is usually established by referring to the electoral roll for that area. The reader receives his membership card or tickets, and the application card is then filed in a register of borrowers.

Some public libraries permit adult readers to become members without guarantors. Most libraries permit residents to register on their own signature, but non-residents may need suitably qualified persons to countersign their application forms. Some libraries may use different forms for the two categories of user, or in some cases different-coloured forms. These forms are then checked against the defaulters' file, which is a list of readers who have failed to return books or refused to pay fines. The application forms are usually valid for three years at a time, and readers may be asked to renew their membership when their tickets expire. The use of coloured tickets can make expiry self-evident. Some libraries send membership cards or tickets to their new readers by post, thus ensuring that the postal information on the application card is correct.

People who work or attend colleges or schools in the area are often permitted to become members at the nearest public library, regardless of where they live. Many library authorities allow readers to use tickets from other authorities at their libraries and this interavailability of membership is very useful, especially when on holiday, although there may be difficulties arising from different issue systems which may be in use.

Changes of address or surname, e.g. on marriage, should be recorded promptly in the readers' register and also on the reader's tickets. From time to time readers may report lost tickets, and each library will have suitable procedures for dealing with this problem. Some may charge a fee for replacement tickets, depending on the method of issue used at that library, for in some cases a missing ticket will correspond to a missing book which may never be recovered.

Bye-laws and regulations

A public library authority may make bye-laws to prevent damage to library premises and their contents and to ensure the proper behaviour of library users. Library bye-laws must be submitted to the Department for National Heritage for confirmation, then printed and prominently displayed. Copies must also be available to the general public on request. People who offend against bye-laws can be prosecuted in magistrates' courts, and may be fined. A set of model bye-laws has been published by the Library Association.

Library regulations do not require confirmation by the DNH and cannot be enforced by law. They usually define how library procedures, such as the loan of materials, are to be carried out so that readers can be treated fairly and consistently. Academic libraries have similar rules to regulate the use of their facilities and services, and they may withdraw membership from those people who persistently refuse to follow them.

Issue systems

Each library will use a system for recording the books or other items it lends to its readers. There have been many modern developments to record issues in the last 30 years, mainly due to the high cost of staffing, increased usage, and in search of better all-round efficiency.

A good system should enable the library staff to discover which reader has borrowed which books. It should show which books are due for return and which are overdue. Some systems can control the number of books issued, and particularly the number which each reader has borrowed. The better system will permit issues to be renewed without returning the book in person, and should allow readers to reserve books which are not immediately available. All these transactions should be done speedily, or else some facility introduced which permits work to be completed later without the reader being kept waiting. Lastly, statistics of various types will be very helpful, and should be capable of collection from the issue system without too much trouble.

Browne

The Browne system of issuing books was used in most public libraries for many years, and is still very common, especially in branch libraries where the volume of issues does not warrant a more sophisticated system.

Each lending book has a bookcard which is kept in a pocket inside each book. The bookcard identifies each book by recording, usually, the accession number, the classification number, author and short title. Each reader has tickets issued which indicate their name and address. This reader's ticket holds the bookcard, which is taken from the pocket in the book, and this forms the record of the issue. Each book is stamped with the date for return and the issue is filed in trays under the date due for return, and within that date probably by accession number.

When the reader returns the book, the date due for return stamped on the date label locates the correct date among the issue trays and the accession number printed on the date label should find the correct position within that date. The bookcard is now returned to the book which is now ready for shelving, and the reader recovers his ticket. If problems occur, the reader is detained until his ticket is found, or until a temporary ticket is prepared. Overdue books are self-evident since the trays are in date order, and reservations are made by searching the issue by date, and then marking the appropriate card in an obvious way.

It is slower to return books than it is to issue them, and over a certain capacity saturation point can be reached where assistants cannot work any faster, and queues begin to form at the library entrance. Unfortunately more assistants do not greatly increase the speed, since they tend to slow each other down, as they each jostle for access to the same trays. The Browne system is easily operated and easily understood by staff and readers alike. It is familiar and has been the most popular and longstanding system in use in Britain. Now, increasing demands have shown that it lacks the capability of dealing with busy periods and consistently large issues. In most central libraries it has been superseded by automated systems.

Computer charging

In recent years, more and more libraries have introduced computerized issue systems to offer improved services for both readers and staff. Computers can deal speedily and accurately with great amounts of data, and can also give instant reserve and overdue facilities which other systems may find difficult to provide.

A typical computer charging system identifies books and readers by barcoded labels, mounted on each book and on readers' cards. A sensing device, usually a light pen, reads the labels and automatically records the information. The date due for return is stamped on the date label, the borrower's card is returned and the transaction is complete. When the book is returned, only the book's barcode needs to be read by the light pen.

Other systems provide book labels which are fixed to the inside back cover of books. A reading head which can penetrate book covers can be used so that books need not be opened, but are merely slid along the counter over the reading device.

Most systems are supplied with trapping stores which contain the numbers of reserved books, and which check each transaction and signal when a reserved book is returned. Book numbers are added to the store or deleted by a numerical keyboard. Trapping stores can also be used to identify specific borrowers when necessary. Renewals are quite simple, requiring book and borrower numbers to be recorded on a keyboard. The trapping store will detect reserves at the renewal stage. Overdue notices are produced by the computer when required. Of course computers can produce an endless variety of statistics based on the data recorded at the issue counter, and a great amount of useful information can be obtained very easily.

Detection devices

Many modern libraries include detection devices at their issue desks to act as a deterrent to would-be thieves. Some systems operate by ensuring that each book is fitted with a trigger, which is a small strip usually attached inside the spine of the book. Triggers are sensitized with automatic equipment, as books are returned. Books which are being taken from the library pass through two detection pillars at either side of the exit. Unless the books have been desensitized, when they were properly issued, they will activate an audio or visual alarm system, which can be fitted to a locking turnstile or door.

Other systems use simple pressure-sensitive labels which incorporate a simple printed circuit and can be quickly fixed onto or inside books and other items to be protected. A very low frequency radio signal activates the label triggers. The manufacturers maintain that their equipment is safe and reliable, and that no commonly carried objects will give false alarms, so that staff may confidently challenge readers whenever necessary. These systems which operate electronically can be effectively incorporated with computer issue systems. When properly installed and operated all systems are highly effective in reducing the theft of library materials.

Public Lending Right

The Public Lending Right Act was passed in 1979 to enable authors to receive payment to compensate for the loss of income incurred as a result of their books being freely available to readers through public libraries in Great Britain. All the money needed to finance Public Lending Right is provided by the Government in a central fund. Authors wishing to draw from this fund must register and claims are assessed according to the number of times their books have been borrowed based on loan records from sample libraries.

Book reservations

When a reader reserves a book, the catalogue should be checked to see if the library holds a copy of the title requested. If so, the shelves should be checked to locate the reserved book, and if the book is on loan, then the appropriate procedure for tracing and stopping the book in the issue should be followed, depending on the system in use. When the book is returned it is held on a reservations shelf and the reader is notified by post that the reserved book is ready for collection.

If the library does not hold a copy, the details should be carefully checked and the union catalogue consulted to make sure that the title is not held elsewhere within the library system, before passing the request to the Interlibrary Loans Section, where the title will be identified by its ISBN or BNB number and a request sent to the local regional library bureau.

Regional library systems

Each library cannot be self-sufficient for all titles or categories of material, and the Regional Library Interlending System was set up, from 1930 onwards, so that participating libraries could draw upon the resources of member libraries when necessary. The country is divided into nine regions including Scotland and Wales (see Figure 2). Within each region, all public libraries and several academic libraries agree to lend material to each other on request. The interlending scheme is administered by a bureau in each region whose function is to maintain a union catalogue of the stocks of all member libraries in the region, and to monitor and allocate requests so that the interlending is spread as evenly as possible among the participating libraries. Requests to the bureau are made on printed forms which are checked against the union catalogue to find locations and are then circulated on a rota to libraries who hold the requested book, until the request is satisfied, or until the list of locations is exhausted. On receiving such a request, a library will check its shelves and issue, supply the requested item by post to the borrowing library, or pass the request to the next library on the list. Requests for urgent material can be made to the bureau by telephone or telex, and an immediate location will be given for the lending library to be approached directly. Some regions have produced ISBN location indexes or even full union catalogues or microfiche, so that member libraries can obtain immediate locations for reserved material. If the bureau is unable to give locations, then the requests will be passed on to the British Library Document Supply Centre, or libraries may apply there in the first place for material which is known to be in short supply in the region, such

National Library
of Scotland

Northern Regional Library System
Cleveland
Cumbria
Durham
Northumberland
Tyne & Wear

Yorkshire & Humberside
Joint Library Services
Humberside
North Yorkshire
South Yorkshire
West Yorkshire

North Western
Regional
Library System
Cheshire
Greater Manchester
Lancashire
Merseyside

Edinburgh

East Midlands
Regional Library
System
Cambridgeshire
Derbyshire
Leicestershire
Lincolnshire
Norfolk
Northamptonshire
Nottinghamshire
Suffolk

BLDSC

Newcastle

West Midlands Regional
Library Bureau
Hereford & Worcester
Salop
Staffordshire
Warwickshire
West Midlands

Boston
Spa

Wakefield

Manchester

Wales Regional
Library Scheme
Clwyd
Dyfed
Glamorgan
Gwent
Gwynedd
Powys

Aberystwyth

Leicester

Birmingham

South West
Regional Library System
Avon
Cornwall
Devon
Dorset
Gloucestershire
Hampshire
Isle of Wight
Oxfordshire
Somerset
Wiltshire

Bristol

London

LASER
Bedfordshire
Berkshire
Buckinghamshire
East Sussex
Essex

Greater London
Hertfordshire
Kent
Surrey
West Sussex

Figure 2   British regional library systems

as foreign material and specialized scientific and technical publications, particularly in serial or report format.

British Library Document Supply Centre

The British Library Document Supply Centre, formerly the British Library Lending Division, is situated in Yorkshire and was established in 1973 by the amalgamation of the National Central Library and the National Lending Library for Science and Technology. Its purpose is to supply libraries speedily with loans and photocopies from stock which are not easily available elsewhere. A large collection has been built up to satisfy this demand, and items not included may be located from other specialist libraries acting as back-up suppliers.

BLDSC is currently building collections of material likely to be needed for interlibrary lending, excluding children's books, fiction and ephemera. Requests are made on prepaid application forms purchased by the borrowing libraries. Part of the purchase price of the application form is to offset delivery and packing charges, and failed requests are refunded. Users may make urgent requests by telephone, telex or fax but a request form identification number must also be quoted.

BLDSC has now produced a catalogue of its current book acquisitions on CD-ROM, and which is also available online through BLAISE-LINE, so that required items can be checked for availability and loan requests can be recorded instantly. This additional service eliminates unnecessary delays and avoids the uncertainties of speculative applications. It is quick, cheap and easy to use.

Loans and photocopies are usually provided within a few days, and are lent for a minimum period of three weeks. Eighty-eight per cent of requests are supplied from stock and a further two per cent from back-up libraries. Average daily requests number 11,000, reaching over three million each year. BLDSC will not accept subject enquiries and the borrowing library is responsible for any bibliographical searching which may be required on behalf of readers. Most requests are supplied by post or via fax, although some regions have direct van service links with BLDSC, ensuring rapid, reliable handling of requests.

Local cooperation

Several cooperative schemes have been established on a local basis in order to provide literature and information quickly and effectively, within well-defined geographical areas. Usually, these local cooperative schemes have developed in response to demands for specialized material from local industry and commerce. A large city reference library or commercial and technical department will frequently form the headquarters, and a catalogue of locations of neighbouring libraries will give locations for requests. Special collections of directories, abstracts and indexes, translation services and sources of periodical holdings will also be provided.

A pioneering scheme was the Sheffield Interchange Organization (SINTO), started in 1933 with specialized subject collections on the steel industry, based on Sheffield City Libraries Commercial and Technical Department. Several other major cities have developed similar schemes, and one other worthy of note is Information North, a development agency for library and information services in the North of England, which undertakes research and development consultancy work; exhibitions, conferences, talks and presentations; and publishes planning papers and a series of health information guides.

Further local cooperative initiatives may include agreements on the cooperative purchase and storage of specialist material, staff training, local transport or computer applications. Often regional bureaux provide bibliographical coordination of local history material such as the North West Sound Archive, and some produce regional bibliographies of local material.

Further reading

British Library Document Supply Centre, *UK customers' handbook*, 6th edn, BL, 1990.

Office of Arts and Libraries, *Current library co-operation and co-ordination*, HMSO, 1986.

McDougall, A.F. and Prytherch, R.J., *Handbook of library cooperation*, Gower. 1991.

Ritchie, S., *Modern library practice*, Elm, 1982.

10

Multi-media and information technology

AV materials

Most libraries will include a selection of material in different formats or media such as audio cassettes, computer software, video tapes, microfiche, illustrations, compact discs, records, slides and cuttings.

Many forms of media cannot be browsed through or scanned like a book or journal, but can only be used by access to equipment or hardware. Each type of material may present problems because of size, physical format, security packaging and storage. They may present problems of retrieval in terms of cataloguing and classification and their bibliographic control is often erratic.

Audiovisual materials are designed to transmit information in different ways, and do not necessarily depend on the printed word to convey their meaning to users. To solve problems with classification and cataloguing and shelving, some librarians have opted to use a modified adaptation of the Dewey system in conjunction with their main central catalogue, but others catalogue AV materials independently of the bookstock. Stocks are either integrated on the shelves, or separated physically but integrated in catalogues. Many libraries cut the cataloguing of AV materials down to the barest minimum, arguing that the simpler the system, the more willingly and more frequently it will be used by borrowers, and it ensures that less staff time is spent on processing or discarding information.

Decisions have to be made as to whether open- or closed-access shelving will be used, i.e. whether items will be in the public areas to be handled at will by borrowers, or whether they should be stored where only the library staff have access. This decision is usually dictated by the format of materials, as each method has advantages and disadvantages.

The advantages of open access tend to favour the potential borrower. Placed in the main part of the library, non-book items are much more likely to catch the attention of library members and, for that reason alone, are much more likely to be readily used. Open access also facilitates the examination of the items, and enables borrowers to browse amongst them. On the other hand, displayed items are more likely to 'disappear' and to become damaged by being more frequently handled.

Closed access enables librarians to store materials in a much more economical way, since items do not have to be displayed for the public. Rooms without windows can be used, and no circulation space for borrowers is required. There is also less potential damage liable to stock. But to store material on closed access does mean that a higher percentage of staff time is spent on the library's cataloguing system, if borrowers are to be kept fully informed of all that is available for loan. Generally speaking, more libraries seem to be moving towards open access for non-book materials, as audiovisual material in particular becomes increasingly available and more cheaply produced.

Information technology

Rapid technological developments have caused librarians to reassess their library stock provision in the light of the demands and needs of modern readers. The need for up-to-date information in industry and commerce has resulted in the creation of a wide range of communications media, and in our homes we are surrounded by a similar range of media for information and leisure. Changes in education have prompted more independent learning and information gathering.

This wide range of materials is due to the explosion of computer, video and telecommunications developments, brought about by the cheapness and availability of modern technological systems and hardware. Often information is easier to understand and interpret when presented visually, and the variety of media and modes of presentation can make valuable contributions, particularly in education where they are used as learning and revision aids.

Computers

Educational libraries have taken the lead in the provision of microcomputers for independent use. The Microelectronics in Education Project set as one of its targets that every school in England and Wales should have access to a computer, and the intention was that all schoolchildren should have a grounding in and hands-on experience of computers. Many college and university libraries now have online public access catalogues, and some public libraries have also prepared catalogues in this way. Small personal computers have become much more powerful, and much cheaper, and we have more computer-literate people than ever before, who are not deterred by using these systems.

College libraries and schools often provide word-processing software packages for use by students who prepare assignments and essays, or tackle problems such as design of questionnaires, preparation of CVs and other work where good presentation is important. There is a wide range of revision software available for testing knowledge and skills in academic subjects. Simple desktop publishing packages are also available to give a professional look to students' work by providing headlines, italics, spacing and so on, when used with laser printers giving high-quality print facilities. Often computers are networked so that software packages, printers and other peripherals can be linked enabling more than one user to share these facilities.

CD-ROM

CD-ROMs are compact discs capable of storing vast amounts of digital data that can be read by laser in a CD-ROM player linked to a microcomputer. CD-ROMs can include text material and audio or visual material. Some discs have combinations of all three, including moving pictures. CD-ROMs are an ideal medium for presenting large volumes of information such as a complete multi-volume encyclopaedia, a year's supply of a daily newspaper, or a bibliographical database on one disk, and this is an easy-to-use and cost-effective way of supplying information.

Two important advantages of CD-ROM as a medium are the increase in the number of access or search factors that can be tried, and the ability to copy selected data electronically. With such large storage capacity available, it becomes necessary to have search software to plough through the mass of data. This is often included on the CD-ROM, although there are variations in how the material is accessed from disk to disk; and from different producers or manufacturers.

One great advantage of CD-ROM is that an international standard (ISO 9660) has been agreed and so manufacturers can produce them knowing they will be universally acceptable, and although there is incompatibility between Apple Macintosh, Acorn and IBM configurations, there are plans to produce multi-format CDs that will run on all these machines in the near future. New developments include improvements to the hardware which could provide everything required in one piece of equipment, and then perhaps portable machines.

CD-ROM facilities are attractive and stimulating to use. They can be very popular in school or college libraries, and this can bring problems of access for large numbers of people needing to use them simultaneously. More computers is not the answer, because only single disks can be used for each stand-alone system. They can be networked to provide greater access but this is expensive.

A range of interactive CD products is now becoming available, and these have exciting new applications for education. In particular, language courses in this medium offer the ability to replay phrases, and refer to vocabularies at the touch of the keyboard, thus keeping the student in control of the pace of the learning experience, with the opportunity to go back and revise or to jump ahead and leave portions to be studied in more depth later.

Online services

Many libraries now have access to online computer databases. All that is required is a microcomputer with the appropriate software, modem, telephone line and permission to access the various databases, which is usually granted on payment of an annual subscription. There are costs involved in consulting such databases and these can be considerable.

BLAISE

The British Library Automated Information Service (BLAISE) is an online service with three functions.

BLAISE-LINE provides bibliographical information on books and audiovisual materials and allows access to British Library records and related databases. The service can be used for checking bibliographical information or for preparing specialist bibliographies. The databases available include the *British Library Catalogue*, *UKMARC* records from the *British National Bibliography*, the *Library of Congress MARC* records, *AVMARC* and *HELPIS*, *Conference proceedings*, *BL Humanities* and *Social Sciences Division*, and *Science Reference and Information Service*, *HMSO* and *UK National Serials Centre* files and the *Whitaker* database of *British books in print*.

Users must pay an annual subscription to BLAISE which covers administration and documentation, and then costs depend on the volume of use. There is an important support and training programme to help users and to keep them up to date with improvements and changes.

ORDER! is an online service which allows users to request material located on BLAISE-LINE from the British Library Document Supply Centre.

BLAISE LINK provides access to a wide range of medical databases originating from the United States National Library of Medicine.

BLAISE LOCAS is a centralized cataloguing service which operates by creating local catalogues by accessing the British Library's cataloguing data online. The value of this resource is its wide range of records, and the integrity of those records in cataloguing terms.

Campus 2000

Campus 2000 is a merger of The Times Network Systems and Prestel Education, and as such has an enormous potential for use in schools and colleges. Users can access a huge variety of information databases, and they can also communicate with other users in the network using electronic mail or computer conferencing facilities.

Campus Prestel is a modified version of British Telecom's Prestel service which is a viewdata service which provides access to information held in the Prestel computers. *Campus Gold* is based on the BT Gold Email service.

Premium services allow Campus 2000 users to access other databases produced and held by other providers. The additional premium services include: *ECCTIS 2000* which supplies information on courses; *PROFILE*, supplying the text of UK newspapers and the *New scientist* for the last three years; *DIALOG classmate* which is a modified version of the international current affairs database for schools; and *SATELLITE* which gives information about BSkyB educational services. *Campus Consultant* provides access to advice and information on Local Management of Schools from the Department for Education. *Campus Teletel* gives access to the French *Minitel* system.

Subscribers must choose the level of subscription they require. Campus gives access to basic services, and Campus Plus gives additional access to Prestel and Premium services.

Teletext

Teletext systems which use a television receiver to communicate information to viewers are being widely adapted for use in industry and business. Teletext is operated from a handset which enables viewers to summon pages of broadcast text information. These systems provide a free source of regularly updated information where currency is important, such as news, financial data, weather, travel, sport, etc. The BBC's teletext service is known as CEEFAX, whilst the ITV services are ORACLE and 4-Tel.

Prestel

Prestel, operated by BT, incorporates the use of a television receiver, keypad and the user's telephone line. In contrast to the teletext services which are one-way, Prestel is an interactive viewdata system using the TV screen to present information and to respond to specific requests from the user. The Prestel computer database stores millions of pages of information and these are being added to and updated continually. A subscriber to the service uses a code index in order to locate the information required. The code is dialled by telephone or input by keypad and the appropriate page of information is displayed on the TV screen. The user can also use the keypad to reply to the system in a limited way. The subscriber is charged for the telephone call, for certain items requested, and for computer time accessing some pages. Almost limitless information can be made available to subscribers, but the system is expensive to use.

Television and video

Many television broadcasts can be recorded for educational use, as a result of the Copyright Designs and Patents Act 1989, and many educational libraries are building up collections of video recordings of educational broadcasts, and other programmes with a documentary or public interest appeal. The Open University allows its broadcasts to be recorded under licence, and so does the Open College. There are also many commercially available video recordings, some specially targeted at the educational market and others such as the BBC Shakespeare series and Dickens' classics which are invaluable for students.

Interactive video is a new medium which has great educational potential. It allows students to select and intervene in the visual process, unlike conventional video. Most interactive video systems are very expensive, and this more than anything has been the greatest obstacle to their wider use.

As cable and satellite broadcasting become more accessible to the general public a much wider range of material will become available for viewing and recording. The potential for educational broadcasting by satellite from abroad, and hence for distance learning at foreign educational institutions, is limitless.

Further reading

CD-ROM, Library Information Technology Centre, 1988 (LIBS, no.3).

Convey, J., *Online information retrieval*, 4th edn, Bingley, 1992.

National Council for Educational Technology, *CD-ROM in schools scheme: evaluation report*, NCET, 1992.

Rowley, J.E., *Computers for libraries*, 3rd rev.edn, LA, 1993.

Stubley, P. and Umney, D., *Multi media*, Library Information Technology Centre, 1992 (LIBS, no.34).

11

Enquiries and reference material

Library assistants may frequently deal with simple reference enquiries. Often they are the first point of enquiry for readers and can gather useful experience of dealing with the public and using reference material in this way. It is important to be familiar with the commoner reference books to be found in most libraries. This familiarity can only be acquired by using and handling such material as often as possible. The contents, coverage, frequency and arrangement should be carefully noted, and any new reference books should be examined as they arrive.

When a reader first makes his enquiry, he should be questioned to discover what is really required. This is often difficult since readers are often unsure themselves, and misleading approaches can waste time for both the assistant and the reader. The reader should be asked if the information is urgent, or if any deadline applies. The assistant must not keep the enquirer waiting unduly, and should take the name, address and telephone number almost at once if the enquirer has telephoned, or if a quick preliminary search indicates that more time will be needed.

The information search should be organized and systematic. The assistant should work from the general to the particular. An encyclopaedia article may provide an initial survey of the subject. The library shelves should be checked for a standard text or a general book containing the subject. If there is no suitable book on the shelves, the library catalogue should be checked for pamphlets, oversize books and added entries. Different approaches via the classification system may be tried, not forgetting special categories of material where applicable, e.g. government publications, trade literature, statistics. Abstracts and periodical indexes should be checked and, if appropriate, newspaper indexes and latest issues. Any appropriate computer databases or viewdata sources, such as Prestel, should also be checked if necessary. The library's own index of difficult queries and information file may also prove useful. Colleagues should be consulted to ensure that all possibilities have been tried. Now that the library's own stock has been covered, it is useful to give the reader an interim report. Sometimes the material already discovered will be sufficient, and sometimes the enquiry may have been satisfied elsewhere in the meantime.

If the enquiry is to proceed beyond the library's own resources, bibliographies and catalogues of other libraries must be consulted. References that have now been gathered, and articles in periodicals not held, can now be obtained through the regional library bureau or the British Library Document Supply Centre. Personal contacts may also be tried. Individual experts, societies, government departments, industrial ·sources may each be approached if applicable, and duly recorded for the next time.

Every book and entry should be recorded to avoid repetition, especially when passing the enquiry on to others. Experienced assistants often get speedy results by different procedures and approaches, but no reader should be left with a negative answer to his enquiry. However, only published authoritative information is required. Personal opinions are only valid where the source is professionally competent, and of course the assistant must never tender such an opinion.

Bibliographies

Bibliographies are lists of books and are compiled in many different forms. They are important for book selection and for finding out about individual books. Authors and titles can be traced and sometimes subject enquiries can be followed. Most libraries will have copies of the basic general bibliographies for British books. Usually they are kept at the readers' adviser's desk, but assistants will need to use them frequently for checking reserves, order cards and simple enquiries.

Books in English records those books listed in the combined Library of Congress and British National Bibliography computer database, and is the largest current bibliography of English-language books published throughout the world. It is an author and title list with full catalogue entries, and Library of Congress and Dewey classification numbers. Each issue is fully cumulated, and is produced every two months on microfiche. Over 100,000 books are listed each year, and there is now a 1971–80 cumulation on microfiche, combining the ten annual listings into a single sequence, and a 1981–5 cumulation. It is as near as possible to being a comprehensive bibliography of English-language books.

The *British national bibliography* started in 1950 and is issued weekly. The preface describes it as 'a list of new British books received by the Copyright Receipt Office of the British Library, arranged according to the 20th edition of the Dewey Decimal Classification and catalogued according to the provisions of the Anglo-American Cataloguing Rules'. It is a comprehensive list of new and forthcoming British books, excluding cheap novelettes, music, maps, minor government publications, and periodicals other than the first issue. It sets out to describe each work in detail, supplying a full catalogue entry, and giving the subject matter of each as accurately as possible. Some entries are prepared from advance information supplied by the publisher, and not from the books themselves. These entries are indicated by the abbreviation CIP (Cataloguing in publication) and advance information on more than 30,000 titles each year is supplied in this way. Each weekly list contains an index of authors, titles and series. Two separate indexes of authors and titles and of subjects covering all items in the weekly lists for each month appear in the last weekly list of the month. There are January to April and May to August cumulations, followed by an annual volume. There is now available a 1950–84 cumulation on microfiche, which covers 35 years of British publishing in a single author-title bibliography, and a 1981–5 complete cumulation with subject-classified entries in addition. It is the authoritative current British bibliography produced by the British Library Bibliographic Services Division. Records from the British National Bibliography are included in the UKMARC (machine-readable cataloguing) files, and can be retrieved via BLAISE and held in computer systems by local libraries, thus avoiding duplication of cataloguing effort.

BNB is also available on CD-ROM as a backfile on two compact disks for the 1950–85 cumulation at a once-only purchase price, and also as a current file since 1986, available by annual subscription in quarterly snowball cumulations. The current file has several new features, including the facility to scan in by light pen the ISBN numbers from the barcodes printed on books to access their catalogue records, and a feature which enables only the latest records added to the quarterly disks to be searched for the very latest material.

British Library also produces *Books at Boston Spa* which records all books published since 1980 which have been acquired from all over the world and which are available for loan via BLDSC. This is available on microfiche, or on CD-ROM. *Boston Spa conferences* is the CD-ROM version of the British Library's *Index to conference proceedings* which lists over 300,000 items, with 18,000 new conferences being added each year. All the items recorded are available for loan through BLDSC. *British reports, translations and theses*, produced monthly by BLDSC, is the most comprehensive record of report literature and doctoral theses available.

Whitaker's books in print is an essential guide to British books available on sale in bookshops each year. It contains a list of British publishers, followed by the main section comprising a combined author and title list of books currently available, whether newly published or not. In printed form *WBIP* contains over 9,500 pages in four volumes, listing over 550,000 titles in print in the UK. Since 1978 *WBIP* has been issued in a microfiche edition, updated and cumulated each month. This gives much greater currency with regard to availability and prices. Each month there are 8,000 new titles added, 5,000 out-of-print titles removed and over 50,000 price alterations. In January and July every year special fiches of *Forthcoming books* are included. Also now available is *Out of print titles on microfiche* listing 300,000 titles published since 1975 which are no longer available. Another additional service is *ISBN listing* issued twice per year, which gives 1,250,000 titles in ISBN sequence with out-of-print books clearly indicated.

WBIP is available on CD-ROM, known as *Whitaker's Bookbank* CD-ROM service. Two important advantages of CD-ROM as a medium are the increase in the number of access or search factors to the book information that can be tried, and the ability to copy selected data from CD-ROM electronically into library computers for use in acquisitions or cataloguing systems. *WBIP* is also available as a computer database which can be accessed online via the British Library's BLAISE-LINE.

Most public libraries subscribe to *The Bookseller*, a weekly trade magazine for the British book industry, which includes a list entitled 'Publications of the week', which is a weekly update of newly published titles. Here, new books including reprints, re-issues and new editions are listed alphabetically under author and title within subject-classified sections. Two large Spring and Autumn preview issues are produced, providing useful advance information about forthcoming books. *Whitaker's books of the month and books to come* is a monthly update of newly published titles, which includes books due for publication in the next two months, and *Whitaker's cumulative book list* is an annual update of all titles published.

The *British catalogue of audio-visual materials* is based on the holdings of the former Inner London Education Authority's Central Library Resources Service. It is published by the British Library Bibliographical Services Division and its arrangement is similar to that of the *British national bibliography*, with a Dewey classified sequence, followed by an alphabetical index of titles, series and names, and an alphabetical subject index. It covers all audiovisual materials except video recordings, 16mm films and musical sound recordings, many of which are listed elsewhere. A second supplement was issued in 1983, but there has been no revision since.

The British Universities Film and Video Council produces a microfiche catalogue of audiovisual materials appropriate for degree-level work, continuing education and in-service training for the professions, covering over 7,000 items from 600 suppliers. This catalogue is compiled from the Higher Education Learning Programmes Information Service (HELPIS) online database, which can be accessed through BLAISE-LINE.

Whitaker's and NCET jointly publish *Educational software*, which is a directory of computer software for primary and secondary schools.

Government publications

British government publications are prepared and issued by Her Majesty's Stationery Office. With an estimated 40,000 titles in print, they form a large and important publishing undertaking, whose subject coverage is wide and varied, except for subjects such as philosophy, religion or pure literature. Tracing official publications can be difficult since only a selection is included in *BNB*, but there are several lists available issued by HMSO to enable customers to identify all their publications quickly and reliably.

The House of Commons *Weekly information bulletin* sets out clearly and concisely a range of detailed, current information on Parliamentary business and publications. It is the only available source for information on the passage of legislation and other new and important topics affecting the business and professional community, as well as the population in general. It is published each Saturday when Parliament is sitting, and is posted to subscribers to arrive on Mondays. The *Sessional information digest* acts in a complementary way to the *Weekly information bulletin*, providing indexes to White Papers and reports of Select Committees.

The *Daily list of government publications* is issued each day except public holidays and weekends and can be posted to libraries daily or in weekly batches. Its five subjects cover Parliamentary papers, non-Parliamentary papers arranged by Ministries and departments, agency publications and statutory instruments which are mainly legal or administrative regulations and all Northern Ireland publications. The *Daily list* is invaluable to those who need to know quickly what is being published by the Government. The *Monthly catalogue of government publications* contains three sections covering Parliamentary papers, a classi-fied list of mainly non-Parliamentary papers and periodicals. It excludes statutory instruments, and has an index of subjects, brief titles and personal names. The *Annual catalogue of government publications* omits statutory instruments and specialized material such as Admiralty charts, Ordnance survey maps, and patents. An annual catalogue of international organizations' publications is issued separately. All HMSO publications in print and avail-able are listed in the quarterly *HMSO in print* on microfiche. Items are included under several headings such as title, author, department and chairman. It is a valuable reference source to the great range of HMSO publications. Current HMSO titles are listed on Prestel on the day they are announced and for a further week, and can be ordered via Prestel. Online access to HMSO's own bibliographic services database is now available through

BLAISE-LINE, and HMSO publications can be sent directly to subscribers by fax, using HMSO's Docufax service.

Other useful guides to British government publications are the *Sectional lists* which are issued free. They cover most government departments, listing the current non-Parliamentary publications of each department, with a selection of Parliamentary papers. The series comprises nearly 30 lists which are regularly revised.

The most famous British government publication is *Hansard's Parliamentary debates* which is a verbatim account of all Parliamentary business. It is published daily while Parliament is sitting, and is cumulated into bound volumes with detailed indexes of subjects and speakers. There is also a weekly *Hansard*. Another well-known publication is *Britain: an official handbook* issued annually by HMSO, which gives outline statistics and basic information on many aspects of British life.

H.M. Government is a valuable and important source of statistical data, and fuller statistical information is available in several publications such as: *Monthly digest of statistics, Annual abstract of statistics, Social trends, Regional trends, Financial statistics,* employment statistics which appear in *Employment gazette,* and of course detailed and nationwide information supplied from the ten-yearly population census.

Periodicals

Periodicals provide up-to-date information and news in advance of books, not only in articles, but in reviews and announcements. More advanced journals are the normal channels for news of research, and many contain the most up-to-date information. Back files of periodicals are often the only source of information on minor topics, and can provide brief summaries for hurried readers. They are often an important source for illustrations which cannot be found elsewhere, and they are the principal source for contemporary opinion of historical events. They are also frequently the only source for information on people and topics that were once well known but are now forgotten.

Guides help to identify and describe periodicals and newspapers. *Current British journals,* which was first published in 1970, is now in its sixth edition. It is produced jointly by BLDSC and the United Kingdom Serials Group, an autonomous body made up of librarians, booksellers, serials agents and publishers, and represents all who are interested in every aspect of serial provision. Entries for about 10,000 British journals are arranged in abridged UDC classified order. Basic information is provided for each title, including the availability of indexes and the existence of microform editions. New features in the latest edition include an index of sponsoring organizations, and an index of ceased titles. There are plans to update the work more frequently.

An important annual British trade guide is *Willings press guide*. It is an alphabetical list of newspapers and periodicals in the United Kingdom, including the year of establishment, the publisher's name and address, price, frequency and day of publication. There is a section classified by subject which is extremely useful. Overseas publications are arranged by country. There is also a newspaper index, a list of UK publishers and their titles, and services and supplies, and a section on new and ceased publications.

Benn's media directory, formerly entitled the *Newspaper press directory*, gives an up-to-date and impartial view of the media scene. Its main sections cover a county/regional index to newspapers, classified indexes to periodicals, directories, agencies and services, and a master A–Z index to all UK publishers. There is an important broadcasting section which covers the BBC, ITC, commercial radio and television, both cable and satellite, and electronic publishing.

The British Library Document Supply Centre produces an annual list of *Current serials received*, which is a title list of over 72,000 journals on all subjects. It includes Cyrillic serials and cover-to-cover translations of Cyrillic serials. Also available from BLDSC on CD-ROM is *Boston Spa serials*, which lists over 300,000 titles accessible from BLDSC including the holdings of other BL Divisions, Cambridge University, and the Science Museum Library, thus creating what is probably the largest database of serial records in existence.

Indexes to periodicals are essential for tracing references and subject enquiries for files which are held elsewhere. The *British humanities index* began in 1962, succeeding the *Library Association subject index to periodicals* which was first published in 1915. It is issued quarterly with an annual cumulation. Periodical articles are indexed alphabetically by subjects, and there is an author index. About 320 British journals are indexed and coverage includes politics, economics, history, literature, philosophy, religion and law. Subsets of *BHI* are now available for women's studies, literature and the environment, bringing together in one sequence the entries on these topics which are scattered in the main work. A sister publication is the *Current technology index*, which began in 1962, and is issued bimonthly, with a cumulated annual volume. Subject headings are arranged alphabetically and there is an author index. Subjects cover all fields of engineering and chemical technology, including the manufactures based upon them. It omits agriculture and medicine. CTI's *Catchword and trade name index* (CATNI) lists alphabetically all names appearing in CTI with full bibliographical references. In 1987, the Library Association began publication of *Applied social sciences index and abstracts* (ASSIA) which provides comprehensive coverage of English-language material – over 550 journals indexed from over 20 countries. Its subject coverage is wide ranging and should prove invaluable for those working in applied social sciences, as well as being extremely useful for those in related fields. *ASSIA* is issued six times per year and there is an annual cumulation.

Library and information science abstracts (LISA) is an abstracting service covering librarianship, information science and publishing. It is international in coverage with over 350 journals from 60 countries. Issued monthly, *LISA* has name and subject indexes, an annual index and a periodicals index.

BHI, CTI, ASSIA and *LISA* were all originally produced by the Library Association. Now they are published and marketed by Bowker-Saur. All four publications are available on CD-ROM, including backfiles. *ASSIA* can be accessed on-line via Data Star, and *CTI* and *LISA* are available through DIALOG.

Current contents reproduces the contents pages of over 7,000 journals each week, and so is a fast, easy and inexpensive way to see what is available in a particular field or journal. *Current contents* is available in seven major subject areas. It is indexed by journal, title word and author, and is also available on diskette in IBM and Apple Macintosh versions, to provide flexible and comprehensive microcomputer searching facilities for subscribers.

Newspapers provide the most up-to-date information and are often the starting-point for readers' enquiries. A national daily and the local newspaper should be taken and held by most libraries. Back files are useful if they are indexed. Indexes to *The Times* have been commercially available for many years, and now indexes to several quality newspapers can be obtained. Many daily newspapers are now available on CD-ROM, which provides electronic browsing and search facilities, with printout options. The quality of text indexing that CD-ROM can offer is now making published indexes less important. CD-ROM equipment can now reproduce photographs and supply printout copies of text from screen.

Keesings record of world events is a digest or summary of news from Britain and overseas, providing impartial and authoritative information on international current affairs. To ensure that the information is as up to date as possible sections are posted to subscribers monthly for insertion in loose-leaf binders, and the arrangement is therefore chronological. There are interim indexes of subjects and names, which are also revised at the end of each year. There is also an annual reference section offering statistical, economic and political information on all countries and international organizations.

Dictionaries and encyclopaedias

Dictionaries give the meaning, spelling and pronunciation of words and are arranged alphabetically. The *Oxford English dictionary* is by far the most comprehensive and detailed English dictionary. It is concerned not only with current usage, but also with the history and development of words. It is now available in a second edition which defines over half a million words, illustrated by over two million quotations, making it more than five times the size of any other English dictionary. The new edition in 20 volumes integrates the original dictionary and its four supplements into one alphabetical sequence which includes an additional 5,000 new words and meanings. The *Oxford English dictionary* is a unique undertaking providing a record of the English language which traces the changing uses of words throughout the centuries. There is a cheaper one-volume compact edition which includes the full text of the new edition read by means of a magnifying glass supplied with a user's guide in a slip case. The *OED* is also available on CD-ROM. The massive database has been compressed onto a single compact disc, requiring an IBM PC 80386 with Windows to operate it. However, the advantages in terms of search factors are enormous, and the data located can be stored or printed to suit the user. The *OED* can also be provided in magnetic tape format using a suitable software retrieval package, and a minimum of 550 Mb hard disk storage.

The *Shorter Oxford dictionary* (2 vols) contains about two-thirds of the words in the main work, and the *Concise Oxford dictionary* is a smaller one-volume edition.

There are many comprehensive one-volume dictionaries, and a typical example is *Chamber's twentieth century dictionary*. This contains entries for 250,000 words and aims to include 'all words in general use in literary and conversational English, plus specialist vocabularies from science, medicine and technology'. The entries include pronunciation, parts of speech, meanings, derivations (phrases and hyphenated forms) and brief etymology. Appendices include lists of foreign phrases, common abbreviations, musical and mathematical symbols and English Christian names. No dictionary is more frequently revised and updated, thus ensuring that it can be relied upon to reflect the language of today.

Roget's thesaurus of English words and phrases gives antonyms and synonyms arranged according to their meanings, or the ideas that they express. For the most effective use the index is essential. A concordance lists all the important words in a particular book and shows where they may be found in that book. *Cruden's complete concordance to the Old and New Testament*, first compiled in 1737, contains over 250,000 entries including all personal and place-names in the Bible.

Encyclopaedias give short accounts of surveys of various subjects, and provide basic factual information. *Hutchinson's new twentieth century encyclopaedia* is a good example of a one-volume encyclopaedia with many short articles, which is also available in CD-ROM format, and *Pear's cyclopaedia* is an authoritative and compact family reference book published annually. The *Macmillan family encyclopaedia* is in 21 volumes with 28,500 articles giving up-to-date information on a vast range of subjects. There are many full-colour illustrations, and almost half the articles have short bibliographies. Arranged clearly in alphabetical order, the index volume refers enquirers to illustrations, captions and maps as well as to the text of articles. The coverage is well balanced with over a third of the work being devoted to science and technology. It is the only multi-volume encyclopaedia to be updated annually.

The *Encyclopaedia Britannica* is an outstanding general encyclopaedia now in its 15th edition. The encyclopaedia is a little confusing to use at first. It is therefore important for assistants to become familiar with its use and arrangement so that readers can be guided when necessary. The first 12 volumes form the *Micropaedia* or ready-reference facility supplying short entries which may lead to more detailed articles in other volumes of the encyclopaedia. The *Macropaedia* in 17 further volumes is the main body of the encyclopaedia giving extended treatment of human knowledge in depth. There is also a one-volume *Propaedia* or outline of knowledge which acts as a study guide to the encyclopaedia. New to this edition is a comprehensive two-volume index providing over 170,000 entries that guide readers with over 400,000 references to information contained in the main encyclopaedia. The *Britannica world data annual* helps to revise the main work, by presenting up-to-date statistics and a review of the previous year's events.

The *Children's Britannica* is now in its fourth edition, providing a huge store of information for homework and projects, well presented and easy for children to use. The *Oxford children's encyclopaedia* has an A–Z sequence in five volumes, with an additional *Biography* volume and index. The science content has been produced in video format for the first time, being available singly, or in a boxed set of three cassettes. The full encyclopaedia has also been published in braille by the National Library for the Blind in 55 volumes.

A typical encyclopaedia of a special subject is the *McGraw-Hill encyclopaedia of science and technology* issued in 20 revised volumes. It is intended 'to provide the widest possible range of articles that will be understandable and useful to any person of modest technical training who wants to obtain information outside his or her particular field of specialization'. It is American in origin and covers the whole field of science and technology, except history and philosophy, and it is simple to understand and use, with up-to-the-minute coverage of all major developments in science.

Two other subject encyclopaedias, despite their titles, are the *Royal Horticultural Society's dictionary of gardening*, and the *New Grove dictionary of music and musicians*. Both are very expensive, authoritative and comprehensive works of scholarship, well illustrated and indexed. Most reference libraries would feel obliged to purchase them to retain their credibility as serious information providers.

Reference books

A reference book is one that is specially arranged and compiled to supply information and facts, rather than to be read continuously. There are many varied types of reference books, and a selection of those which might be found in most libraries is described here.

The *Guinness book of records* is one of the most successful reference books ever devised, and it is most popular with children. Its contents are arranged into 12 parts, and there is a strong emphasis on sporting information. There are many illustrations and a good index.

Whitaker's almanack is an annual publication giving general information. It is an encyclopaedia, a directory and an annual survey rolled into one. Particularly important is the review of political, scientific, sporting and cultural events of the preceding year. No single book contains as much information, although much of it is often very brief, and it is usually the first checkpoint for general reference enquiries.

The *Statesman's yearbook* is an annual reference book on the countries of the world containing an outline of political, economic, cultural and statistical information, including industries, natural resources, a bibliography and diplomatic representatives. It is arranged in two parts: *International organizations*, including the United Nations and its agencies, and *Countries of the world*, arranged alphabetically.

The standard reference book for local government in the United Kingdom is the *Municipal year book*. It reviews the previous year's work, then lists all local authorities giving details such as population, area, finance, members, chief officers, in addition to statistical tables on local government activities such as housing and education. The index is at the front, and there are sections on public services, government departments, and development corporations.

Dun and Bradstreet's *Key British enterprises* lists 50,000 top UK companies, supplying information on people to contact in each firm, financial details, operational information and corporate details. The companies are listed alphabetically, by industry and geographically.

Croner's provide up-to-date loose-leaf information services on a wide range of legal and administrative matters for those in business and the professions, e.g. *Guide to health and safety at work*, *Industrial relations law*, *Reference book for exporters*, and *Croner's Europe*. They aim to provide comprehensive and authoritative information which is practical and easy to understand. The loose-leaf format ensures that the information is as up to date as possible.

Kelly's business directory is an annual reference work recognized throughout the world as the leading buyer's guide to British industry and commerce. It includes the name, address, telephone number and trade description of over 82,000 organizations engaged in industry and commerce in the UK. It includes a large classified section with over 15,000 trade and professional headings. There is a specialist section on the oil and gas industry, and one on international exporters which is indexed in four languages.

Kompass UK lists the suppliers of 44,000 products and services arranged within the main industrial groups, and gives company information arranged geographically. There is a volume giving financial data, another on parents and subsidiaries which identifies a company's position within the complete corporate structure, and another on industrial trade names.

Kelly's Post Office London business directory has a company information section providing an alphabetical guide to businesses within the London area, a full-colour street atlas, a street section listing businesses numerically under 65,000 streets, and sections on local authority departments and official information. The classified trades section arranges 80,000 businesses under 8,000 trade headings including London's legal, financial and property services, and there is a cross-referenced index to all trade classifications.

Telephone directories should not be ignored. They are useful sources of information on addresses and trade enquiries. They also supply details such as correct postal addresses and emergency services. Classified directories and *Yellow pages* include entries under trades, manufacturers and professions. There is no other reference book which is more taken for granted.

Kempe's engineer's year book is produced annually and supplies information for all engineering enquiries. There are 85 chapters with 3,500 pages of information grouped into 12 principal sections of interrelated subjects covering all areas of engineering. There are 2,000 technical illustrations and diagrams, and over 800 tables and graphs supplying essential figures and data. Comprehensive bibliographies follow each chapter, and there is a detailed 80-page index.

The *Medical directory* is a register of up-to-date information on over 120,000 doctors registered to practise medicine in the UK. There is also a useful local area list to locate doctors by the city or town where they live or practise. It contains a complete list of all hospitals, health authorities and boards including details of consultants and their specialities. Also included is a list of teaching and research institutions, medical societies and associations, coroners and Royal appointments.

The *Dictionary of national biography* is the most important retrospective reference work of English biography. It is issued in 22 volumes with supplements up to 1985. It contains lengthy signed articles with good bibliographies. The *Concise DNB* in three volumes has brief versions of all the entries and serves as both a summary and an index to the main work. There is also a new *DNB missing persons*, covering over 1,000 people who have become famous posthumously, or who were never included in the original work. *Who's who* is the leading British biographical dictionary of living people, with approximately 30,000 entries. People are included for their personal achievement or prominence and interest to the public at large. Entries are compiled from information provided by the subjects themselves and include full name, description, date of birth, children, education, activities, publications, recreations, dates and telephone numbers. There is additional information on the Royal Family, the New Year's Honours List, a list of abbreviations, and an obituary.

Who was who is a compilation of those people who were originally included in *Who's who*, and have now died.

Atlases and gazetteers

Atlases are bound volumes of maps, charts and tables, which are essential for the study of geography and may also be useful for information on current affairs. *The Times atlas of the world* is a comprehensive and reliable reference work with over 130 maps, and with an index on world resources.

Gazetteers give the location of places, together with appropriate economic or historical information. *Bartholomew's gazetteer of places in Britain* has 40,000 entries and gives National Grid references. It includes place-names created during local government reorganization in Great Britain.

Motoring handbooks contain lists of towns and provide details of hotels, garages, population and early closing days. They contain detailed road maps and town plans, and supply full information of the services offered to members. The *Royal Automobile Club handbook* is issued annually and is generally available; the *Automobile Association handbook* is for members only.

AA big atlas of town plans is an atlas covering 64 major towns and cities in Britain with many clear plans covering town centres, suburban main routes, central London and airport plans. It shows one-way systems, parking facilities, and principal shopping areas.

Information file

Every library should have its own information file which should contain, among other details, the addresses and telephone numbers of local council offices, government departments, local chambers of commerce, associations, societies, churches, schools, travel offices, police stations and emergency services. In fact, all or any local information thought to be useful which is not readily available elsewhere should be immediately accessible here. Not all the reference books mentioned here will be available in every library, but most should be. The efficient library assistant will know that they exist and will know how to locate and use them when necessary.

Further reading

Higgens, G., *Printed reference material and related information sources*, 3rd rev. edn, LA, 1990.

Jackaman, P., *Basic reference and information work*, 2nd rev.edn, Elm, 1989.

Katz, W.A., *Introduction to reference work*, 2 vols, 6th rev. edn, McGraw-Hill, 1992.

Ollé, J.G. and Dixon, D., *Guide to sources of information in libraries*, 2nd edn, Gower, 1991.

Walford, A.J. et al., *Walford's Guide to reference material*, 3 vols, 5th rev. edn, LA, 1989–91.

12

Office practice

All clerical workers need to be both tidy and methodical in their work. there are special reasons why it is even more important for library assistants to practise neatness and orderliness in carrying out their clerical duties.

Library assistants carry out duties in many areas of the library, according to the nature of the task in hand. They work intermittently on clerical duties, whilst at the same time staffing issue desks and attending to readers. Most libraries have a longer working day than the average office, and to cover the long opening hours, including the evening sessions, it is necessary to organize staff timetables on a variable shift system. This can result in work being started by one assistant and completed by another. Since many clerical duties are carried out in the public sector of the library, this means that work is frequently interrupted to attend to readers. For all these reasons careful thought has to be given to setting up clerical working space, to procedures for when work is interrupted, or has to be left for someone else to complete, and also to leaving the working area in good order when the task is finished.

Any items of equipment that have been used should be carefully returned to their places, so that the next user does not waste time searching for them. Above all, particularly for on-coming part-time staff, precise messages and clear instructions should be left to ensure continuity and to prevent confusion.

Post

Most libraries will have a postal delivery each day, and some will have such large amounts of post to deal with that it becomes important to establish regular procedures for handling and sorting post in a consistent and orderly manner. The post must be attended to early in the day, because many of the items delivered may affect the work of the library and need to be distributed internally as soon as possible.

Envelopes marked 'confidential', 'personal', or 'private' should not be opened, but should be delivered intact. Other items should be opened carefully and their contents unfolded. Any enclosures should be neatly attached, any cheques or postal orders promptly recorded, and each item delivered should be date-stamped and initialled. All items should now be sorted under their appropriate headings. Inter-library loans, periodicals, lending enquiries and administrative post should all be separated and distributed to the departments concerned. Finally, the empty envelopes should be checked to see that nothing has been missed, before clearing away.

Outgoing post should be separated into external and internal. Internal post will be distributed according to local arrangements, and external post through the normal Post Office services. Letters and parcels should be separated, and then each stamped with the correct postage values. Large libraries may use franking machines for this, if the volume of post is sufficient. Library postal assistants should become familiar with the full range of Post Office services, set out in the *Post Office guide*, which should be readily available. In particular, staff should know the correct charges for parcels, printed papers, recorded delivery and express services.

Telephones

Just as library assistants working at the issue counter help to create a good impression of the library, so does the handling of telephone calls and callers. Many new telephone systems are now being installed with a range of facilities such as redirecting calls to other extensions, so that calls are not lost. Enquiries should be dealt with promptly, courteously and efficiently at all times. A notepad and pen should be available next to each telephone so that staff are ready to deal with calls immediately. When answering calls always give the name of your library and of your department clearly and deliberately, and follow this with a greeting. Identify your caller correctly and write down the name, date and time of the call. Listen to what the caller says and make brief notes. Ask for further details, if the information given is not sufficient, and then read back to the caller the message you have written down. If the caller has to be kept waiting, give reassurances from time to time, so that he has not been cut off, or simply ignored. Finally, if the query cannot be dealt with immediately, write down the caller's own telephone number, offer to ring him back; and where necessary outline the steps that will be taken in the meantime.

Electronic mail

Electronic mail is a system of communication between computers or terminals linked by telephone lines. Messages are sent via a keyboard to destinations which are identified by numbered codes. The message is thus held in a central computer postbox until the recipient calls up the number to see if there are any messages waiting. Messages can then be read from a visual display unit, down loaded onto disk or printed out onto paper if necessary. Only the person with the identification code number can receive the mail.

Computer messages are transmitted by telephone via a modem which converts the information into digital signals. The central computer holding the information until it is required can supply additional facilities such as simultaneous transmissions to several destinations, and delayed timing to take advantage of off-peak charges. *Telecom Gold* is a large, national system run by British Telecom offering many of these message handling facilities which may be quite expensive to use. Many school and college libraries will have access to Campus 2000 at reduced rates for educational use.

Subscribers to E-mail are offered a combination of the best features of the telephone and the typewriter; speed plus the authority of the printed word. Users are able to send and receive virtually any form of printed message.

Telephone callers may be misunderstood, but electronic mail gives a written message which can be referred to whenever necessary. Moreover, the receiving end does not need to be manned constantly, for messages can be stored over a weekend or during evenings until required.

Electronic mail can be used by libraries to supply information in answer to requests from other users. It can be used to communicate with other libraries for interlending and other purposes. It is a quick and accurate method of corresponding with any other organization that also subscribes.

Fax

Facsimile transmission allows an exact copy of a document to be transmitted over a telephone line, thus enabling complicated diagrams, graphs, tables of statistics, or pictures to be sent to a given destination in a matter of minutes.

This can be very useful in libraries for interlibrary lending. BLDSC offers an urgent fax service, and obviously this is very popular with readers who can obtain facsimile copies of material requested, almost while they wait.

Many fax machines incorporate answerphones which can be useful for recording messages, such as issue renewals, when the library is closed. Staff will process these messages each morning and make the necessary adjustments to the issue. It adds up to a much improved and more convenient service to the user, if services and facilities are available around the clock.

Office machinery

In modern offices a range of clerical and administrative work is increasingly aided by the use of office equipment of different kinds. Where the work is routine or repetitive, office equipment can save considerable time and effort on the part of office workers. Often the accuracy and quality of work produced is improved, and the appearance of written and numerical work is enhanced.

Almost every library office will contain a typewriter for general as well as specifically library clerical work. There are many makes and sizes of typewriter depending on the kind of work required. Most modern offices use electric typewriters which are less tiring for their operators, and give an evenness of touch which improves the quality of carbon copies or duplicated stencils. Electric variable typewriters which offer interchangeable sizes and styles of type can also be obtained. Line and word spaces can be adjusted so that the finished work looks very similar to letterpress printing. Some modern typewriters have miniature display screens so that users can see what they have typed before printing. Some also have small electronic memories for storing information that is frequently used, such as names and addresses of suppliers, which can then be included without keyboarding them on every occasion they are required.

Word processors allow numbers, letters or words to be retained in a computer style memory so that they can be altered, rearranged or edited after they have been typed. Characters are typed on a keyboard and projected on to a screen called a *visual display unit*, so that the operator can correct or rearrange what is shown before the final version is printed. Word processors are used mainly for repetitive work with uniform contents which can be made to appear individual or distinctive by the addition of names and addresses or other personal details, or for preliminary versions of letters, minutes and reports which can be easily amended or revised.

Software is now available that can check spelling and punctuation for accuracy, and then correct typing mistakes! Many word-processing machines are specially designed for this purpose, but word-processing programs can be obtained for use with most microcomputers with sufficient memory capacity to be viable.

Desktop publishing (DTP) software is available for use with high-quality laser printers to give good-quality design and print facilities for library publications or promotional material.

Electronic office

In a modern, automated office, staff may work at computer terminals linked together and to a central computer providing information for use by everyone. For instance, the record that is created when a book is ordered can be stored for use again when that book is catalogued, and again when it is issued, rather than separate records being created for each purpose. Each computer terminal can use software to deal with the same information in different ways. Some libraries now have public access systems which allow readers to access computer catalogues and issue systems online to search for material, or make issue enquiries.

Computers can use and rearrange information very quickly, and they bring an accuracy and consistency that takes much of the drudgery out of routine operations such as filing in alphabetical order, writing overdues and addressing envelopes for mailing lists. Unfortunately computers still cannot clear tables and shelve books!

Photocopying

Photocopying machines provide exact copies of original material. They are frequently used for copies from books and journals, as well as for diagrams, charts and normal office copying. Most photocopying machines are easy to use, and are quick and cheap for small numbers of copies. Some machines use a photographic process for which special fluids or papers are required, and these can be messy and inconvenient. Other machines require the original document to enter and pass through the machine, and these of course are unsuitable for library copying.

Electrostatic copiers are becoming increasingly popular in offices and libraries. Copies are produced directly on to ordinary paper by an electric charge, and there are no fluids or negatives involved. Xerography is one of the commonest electrostatic processes. Often machines are supplied on rental. All photocopying machines need careful usage, and regular cleaning and maintenance. The number and types of copies taken should be recorded, and regular checks made on the amount of stationery or supplies needed.

Many photocopying machines are now provided for self-service use by readers, either coin operated or by purchasing photocopy cards. Some machines are capable of magnifying or reducing copies, and these are useful for notices where the information can be typed and then enlarged to the required size. Full-colour copiers are also available.

Copyright

The law of copyright has recently been revised by the Copyright Designs and Patents Act 1989, to take account of the increase in technology and facilities available with regard to photocopying, and the role and use of audio and video recording equipment and materials, and also to extend similar legal protection to computer software.

Briefly, as the law now stands with regard to photocopying in public libraries in Great Britain, only single copies can be supplied for the purpose of research or private study, on payment of a fee, 'not less than the cost (including a contribution to the general expenses of the library) attributable to their production'. Readers who require copies should be asked to

METROPOLITAN
BOROUGH OF STOCKPORT

STOCKPORT *college*
OF FURTHER & HIGHER EDUCATION

WELLINGTON ROAD SOUTH
STOCKPORT SK1 4UQ

Copyright declaration re: Copyright Act 1988

To: College Librarian

Name...

Faculty...

Please supply me with one copy of:-
(please quote full reference)

....

....

....

....

....

....

I declare that:-

a) I have not previously been supplied with a copy of the same material by you or any other librarian.

b) I will not use the copy except for research or private study and will not supply a copy of it to any other person.

c) To the best of my knowledge no other person with whom I work or study has made or intends to make, at or about the same time as this request, a copy of substantially the same material for substantially the same purpose.

I UNDERSTAND THAT IF THE DECLARATION REGARDING THIS MATERIAL IS FALSE I SHALL BE LIABLE FOR INFRINGEMENT OF COPYRIGHT AS IF I HAD MADE THE COPY MYSELF.

Signature...................................

Date   ....

REFERENCE	
COPIES	
TOTAL COST	

Figure 3   Specimen photocopy application form

sign a copyright undertaking (Figure 3) and should be charged the appropriate fee before the copying is done.

Many local authorities have taken out licences with the Copyright Licensing Agency on behalf of the schools under their control. This permits multiple copies of copyright material to be made for educational purposes on payment of an annual fee. There are many exclusions to the licence, e.g. newspapers.

Data protection

The Data Protection Act 1984 is concerned with personal information stored and processed by computers. Individual persons are given certain rights by the Act, and computer users must observe obligations which are described as Data Protection Principles. The Principles stipulate that personal data:

- a) shall be obtained and processed fairly and lawfully;
- b) shall only be stored for specified and lawful purposes, and shall not be used for any other purposes;
- c) shall be adequate, relevant and not excessive for the purpose it is held;
- d) shall be accurate and kept up to date;
- e) shall not be kept longer than necessary.
- And f) Individuals are entitled to access any personal information about them, and to have this data corrected or erased.
- g) Security measures must be taken to prevent unauthorized access to such information.

All computerized personal information and its uses must be registered with the Data Protection Registry so that persons may gain access to information about themselves which is held in computer systems. It is a criminal offence to misuse personal data and individuals may be entitled to compensation if damage is caused by inaccurate information or unauthorized disclosure of such information.

Data security requirements for libraries should include the physical security and access to computer equipment, software security including the use of passwords and restrictions on access to sensitive data, and working practices such as the storage and disposal of printout materials. Personal information which staff may obtain in the course of their work is confidential, and disclosure of such information to unauthorized persons is a very serious matter.

Microreaders

Microreaders are machines to enable the different kinds of microforms to be magnified for reading. There should be machines available for reading every kind of microform held by the library. In a large library this will include 35mm and 16mm roll film, microfiche and microcard. Microreading equipment is not complicated, and library staff should be familiar with its use, and particularly with the interchanging of bulbs, lenses and other carriage components needed for reading the different formats. Many machines are now modified to accept roll film in cassette form, which simplifies usage, and eliminates threading. Some machines have motorized winding and instant photocopying facilities.

Audiovisual equipment

In educational libraries especially there may be collections of audiovisual material for use by readers. All the necessary audiovisual equipment should be available for use with each type of material held (with the appropriate monitors and playing equipment). Complicated equipment which allows random access to recorded information, or online computer databases with elaborate protocols or even microcomputers on open access may present problems for members of the public, and therefore all library staff should be properly trained to operate all the equipment available and to anticipate simple software problems. They should also be able to perform simple, routine maintenance such as replacing ribbons, or setting up paper printers, in order to provide a fully comprehensive range of services and assistance to readers at all times.

Further reading

Barcomb, D., *Office automation*, 2nd rev.edn, Digital Press, 1989.
Library Association, *Guidelines on copyright in:*
  Industrial and commercial libraries
  NHS libraries
  Polytechnic and university libraries

Public libraries
School and college libraries
Mullins, E., *Electronic office equipment*, Pitman, 1987.
Stanwell, S.T., *Office practice*, 4th rev. edn, Arnold, 1989 [1976].

General reading

Bunch, A., *The basics of community information work*, LA, 1993.

Harrison, C. and Beenham, R., *The basics of librarianship*, 3rd rev. edn, Bingley, 1990.

Harrison, K.C., *First steps in librarianship*, 5th rev. edn, Gower, 1980.

Lock, R.N., *Manual of library economy*, Bingley, 1977.

Prytherch, R.J., *Librarian's glossary of terms used in librarianship ... and reference book*, 7th rev. edn, Gower, 1990.

Ritchie, S., *Modern library practice*, 2nd rev. edn, Elm, 1982.

Rowley, J.E., *The basics of information technology*, Bingley, 1987.

Anyone wishing to keep up to date with developments in libraries should see copies of the following periodicals regularly:

The assistant librarian

Audiovisual librarian

Library Association record

New library world

The Library Information Briefing Series prepared by the Library Information Technology Centre should also be consulted regularly.

INDEX